ECUMENICAL STUDIES IN WORSHIP

No. 8

THE
EUCHARISTIC MEMORIAL

by

MAX THURIAN

Sub-Prior of the Community of Taizé, France

PART II—THE NEW TESTAMENT

Translated by

J. G. DAVIES

JOHN KNOX PRESS

Richmond, Virginia

Library Congress Catalog Card No. 61-5399

ECUMENICAL STUDIES IN WORSHIP

CONTENTS

3

First published 1961

© 1959 DELACHAUX & NIESTLÉ, S.A., NEUCHÂTEL (SWITZERLAND)
ENGLISH TRANSLATION © 1961 LUTTERWORTH PRESS
4 BOUVERIE STREET, LONDON, E.C.4

This volume consists of a translation of Part II of Max Thurian, *L'Eucharistie, Mémorial du Seigneur, Sacrifice d'action de grâce et d'intercession* (Delachaux and Niestlé, Neuchâtel and Paris, 1959), with the addition of an extended note on pp. 84 f. and with the alteration of the text of the eucharistic prayer printed in the Appendix to conform with that in *Eucharistie à Taizé*, 1959, pp. 15–18.

Part I, *The Eucharistic Memorial: The Old Testament*, has been published as a separate volume in this series.

A translation of the Taizé Eucharistic Liturgy, with introduction by Max Thurian, is published by the Faith Press, London.

*Printed in Great Britain by
Latimer, Trend & Co., Ltd., Plymouth*

I

THE MEMORIAL IN THE NEW TESTAMENT

THE WORD ἀνάμνησις is used three times in the New Testament to designate the eucharistic memorial (Lk. 22: 19; 1 Cor. 11: 24, 25); it is also found in several other passages, with its synonym μνημόσυννον (Heb. 10: 3; Acts 10: 4; Matt. 26: 13; Mk. 14: 9), to designate a non-eucharistic memorial, but even in these instances it is still to be understood against the background of the Old Testament tradition, which has been examined in Part I of this study. An examination of these various New Testament passages will shed further light upon the meaning of memorial in general and upon that of the eucharistic memorial in particular.[1]

The Memorial of Sin to obtain Forgiveness

First to be considered is the passage in the Epistle to the Hebrews which contains the word *anamnesis*. This is the first part of the tenth chapter, in which the argument of the Epistle is most clearly presented. The priesthood of Christ has been shown to be superior to the priesthood of the old covenant, and in this chapter the ineffectiveness of the ancient sacrifices is affirmed, "a shadow of the good things to come", in comparison with the unique sacrifice of Christ, which alone is effective for the forgiveness of sins. The repetition of the sacrifices for sin proves that they are not effective. "Else would they not have ceased to be offered, because the worshippers, having been once cleansed, would have had no more conscience of sins? But in those sacrifices there is a remembrance made of sins year by year" (10: 2 f.). There is here an undoubted reference to Aaron's confession over the scape-goat (Lev. 16: 21) and to the meal offering of jealousy (Num. 5: 15). This sacrifice for sin, referred to in Hebrews, is a kind of solemn confession before God and before the people, intended to recall their sin to men with a view to repentance and to recall it to God with a view to judgment. The Israelites hoped for a merciful judgment; actually,

[1] For ἀνάμνησις see *Th.Wb.N.T.*, I, pp. 351-52; and for μνημόσυννον *ibid* IV, pp. 685 ff.

5

according to the author of the Epistle, this judgment is now a condemn-ation, because remission of sins is obtainable only through the sacrifice of Christ. The sacrifices of the old covenant can be compared only with the meal offering of jealousy, recalling sin to men that they may burn with shame, and recalling it to God who allots punishment. The meal offering of jealousy was a "meal offering of memorial, bringing iniquity to remembrance" (Num. 5: 15). The memorial of sin in the ancient sacrifices has exactly this meaning: "to attract the attention of Yahweh to the sinner's misdemeanour that He may not forget to chastise him."[1] This is a dramatic and pessimistic conception of the Jewish cultus which, because of Christ's sacrifice, is regarded as having no positive effect.

The word *anamnesis* therefore, in this passage, expresses a recalling before God; it bears the meaning that has already been defined and which it shares with its synonym *mnemosunon*.[2] This remembrance of God that He may chastise is also referred to in Revelation (16: 19) in terms which suggest the memorial *before* God: "Babylon the great was remembered in the sight of God (Acts 10: 4, 31), to give unto her the cup of the wine of the fierceness of his wrath."

If the Jewish sacrifices only recall the sin before God and if the sin of Babylon is recalled before Him that she may be punished, in Christ and because of His sacrifice God remembers only His mercy. "I will forgive their iniquity, and their sin will I remember no more": this promise, in Jeremiah 31: 34, is quoted twice by the author of Hebrews (8: 12; 10: 17). And Christian prayer can assert with complete con-fidence, with Mary in the *Magnificat* and with Zacharias in the *Bene-dictus*:

> He hath holpen Israel his servant,
> That he might remember mercy . . .
> To shew mercy towards our fathers,
> And to remember his holy covenant (Lk. 1: 54, 72).

The passage in Hebrews under consideration, containing the word "memorial", also raises an important problem which is directly con-cerned with our study of the Eucharist. The fundamental theme of the

---

[1] C. Spicq, *L'Epître aux Hébreux*, II, 1953, p. 103. With Farrar, Westcott, Windisch and Moffatt, Spicq establishes the connexion of this text with the meal offering of jealousy.

[2] "Ἀνάμνησις is not any sort of remembrance, either subjective or entirely inward (μνήμη, μνεία), but a recalling, a manifestation—by word or deed—which compels the recalling of the past, *commemoratio*", Spicq *loc. cit.*

whole section may be summarized thus: the old covenant does not possess the substance of reality; its sacrifices therefore can only recall sin and not remit it; its priests therefore act ineffectively as they minister at the daily sacrifices. On the other hand, Christ is the image of the divine substance; His unique and perpetual sacrifice has remitted sin; Christ, the everlasting Priest, is therefore seated at the right hand of God and awaits in peace the fulfilment of His work in time.

Two questions arise about the problem of the Eucharist: can Christ be considered as a Priest now, and can the Eucharist be considered as a sacrifice?

No doubt a contrast is intended between the vain posture of the Jewish priests, standing to officiate, and the peaceful posture of Christ, sitting in calm expectation (10: 11 f.). Must we then conclude that the author of Hebrews thinks that the priesthood of Christ on the cross came to an end when He sat down at the right hand of God? If so, then this passage would contradict chapter 7 which applies Ps. 110: 4 to Christ: "Thou art a priest for ever, after the order of Melchizedek" (7: 17, 21). Christ, "because he abideth for ever, hath his priesthood unchangeable" (7: 24). The passage continues: "wherefore also he is able to save to the uttermost them that draw near unto God through him, seeing he ever liveth to make intercession for them" (7: 25). Christ has entered heaven "now to appear before the face of God for us" (9: 24). This last expression indicates the character of Christ's everlasting priesthood and reintroduces the idea of the memorial. Christ is Priest to eternity in so far as He presents before the face of the Father the image of His unique and perfect sacrifice; His present priesthood is a priesthood of intercession extending the sacrificial priesthood of the cross, with which it is one. The contrast between the Jewish priests standing and Christ sitting means no more than that the priesthood of Christ is not an agonized and troubled ministry; it is accomplished in the peace of Him who has obtained everything in advance, and who has nothing further to do but to present His perfect sacrifice as an act of intercession which is certain to be granted.[1]

The second question is whether the assertion that Christ's sacrifice is unique prevents us from describing the Eucharist as a sacrifice. The word ἐφάπαξ, "once for all", which is found three times in Hebrews (7: 27; 9: 12; 10: 10), emphasizes the unique and final character of the

---

[1] It may be recalled that St. Stephen beheld the Son of Man "standing on the right hand of God" (Acts 7: 56). We must therefore not split hairs over these questions of posture which relate only to interior attitudes.

sacrifice of Christ upon the cross, of His entry into the heavenly sanctuary and of the sanctification of the people of God. The adjective "one" or unique is twice applied to the sacrifice in chapter 10 (vv. 10, 12). This is one of the essential themes of the letter: by means of a unique sacrifice offered on the cross (7: 27), borne into heaven in intercession (9: 12), Christ has accomplished the forgiveness of sins and the sanctification of His people (10: 10, 12). If this great sacrifice, which extends from the cross to heaven, was accomplished once for all in a unique and perfect manner, it has an everlasting character because of Christ's intercession, who is "now to appear before the face of God for us" (9: 24). The verb ἐμφανίζω, to appear, to make visible, to make known, to manifest, signifies an active presence of Christ; in a more technical sense it means "to draw attention to a petition, to make an official report". Thus the expression refers quite clearly to the intercession of Christ; "He represents those who have been summoned, He takes their cause in hand and pleads it . . ."[1] And this is accomplished by Him now, i.e. the intercession of Christ, based upon His sacrifice, endures until the Parousia. Hervé de Bourgdieu's commentary on this is worthy of quotation: "He appears before the face of God, that is in the presence of the all merciful Father: He intercedes for us with Him, showing the marks of His wounds which He has borne for our redemption, and He presents everlastingly all that He has endured for our salvation."[2] There is therefore a unity and a perpetuity of the priesthood and sacrifice of Christ in two modes, that of the cross and that of heaven. "His priestly mediation continues in heaven under a new mode and makes the most of the sacrifice of the cross. . . . Henceforth the high priest is present before God and officiates now on behalf of His own."[3]

The term "once for all" should not therefore be understood to have a static meaning relating only to the past. The word rather signifies the absolute, complete and everlasting character of Christ's sacrifice; it does not imply a unique moment with no effects under different modes which recall it and make it present. Another Greek phrase, εἰς τὸ διηνεκές, continually or for ever, sheds light on the adjective "unique" and the phrase "once for all". It is used four times in Hebrews. First, in connexion with Melchizedek, it is the equivalent of "to eternity". If Melchizedek is said to be a priest "continually" or "to

[1] Spicq, op. cit., p. 268.
[2] Quoted by Spicq, op. cit., p. 268.
[3] Ibid.

eternity", it is because he is assimilated to the Son of God and is not merely an individual who once lived in the past. His priesthood existed in one mode at the time of Abraham, in another in Christ on the cross, and in a third in Christ in heaven. The continuity of Melchizedek's priesthood is expressed, in its unity, under different modes. The same expression is used of the continual and vain repetition of the Jewish sacrifices (10: 1). It also qualifies the sacrifice of Jesus Christ (10: 12) and the consecration which has been achieved for the people of God (10: 14). "He, when he had offered one sacrifice for sins for ever (continually), sat down on the right hand of God" (10: 12). The sacrifice of the cross, qualified in this way, appears as an act which is unique, not in the sense that it will not appear again in any form but as the origin and source of a continual work which is the remission in Christ of the sins of all those who approach God through Him. The sacrifice of the cross is thus extended in the heavenly intercession of Christ until the Parousia. The uniqueness of Christ's sacrifice does not imply an isolated act in past history but an historical act with a continuing efficacy which is extended in the intercession of the Son of God: the unique sacrifice of Christ on the cross is an everlasting sacrifice which gathers together all the sacrifices, prayers and deeds of the people of God in the unity of His present and living intercession.

"For by one offering he hath perfected for ever them that are sanctified" (10: 14). Here the fruit of the sacrifice is being considered. By His sacrifice Christ has brought the salvation of men to fulfilment. If salvation is accomplished in Christ, if we are sure to be saved by faith in Him, a work of sanctification is continued in us. This must not be understood in a moral sense; it does not refer to a perfecting of holiness but to the accomplishing of a consecration. In the Pentateuch, according to the Greek version, this verb is used of the consecration of the High Priest when he enters upon the fullness of the priesthood. "Thou shalt put the whole upon the hands of Aaron, and upon the hands of his sons" (Ex. 29: 9, 24, 29, 33, 35; Lev. 4: 5, 8, 33; 16: 32; 21: 10; Num. 3: 3). This meaning is clearly to be found in Hebrews when the verb "to perfect" is used of Christ. "For it became him, for whom are all things, and through whom are all things, in bringing many sons unto glory, to make the author of their salvation perfect (consecrated) through sufferings . . . And having been made perfect (consecrated), he became unto all them that obey him the author of eternal salvation; named of God a high priest after the order of Melchizedek . . . for the law appointeth men high priests, having infirmity; but the word of the oath, which was after the law, appointeth a Son, perfected (consecrated) for evermore" (2:10; 5:9 f.; 7:28). When therefore Hebrews refers to God perfecting Christ, what is in mind is a fulfilment in the High Priesthood, a solemn consecration by suffering. Christ is brought by the Father not to a greater moral or spiritual perfection (He is holy), but to a fulfilment or completion of His priesthood, to a consecration which defines the function of the High Priest for ever: "He will exercise His priestly functions in heaven".[1]

For Christians also "making perfect" is in the first instance a priestly consecration. In the verse following that which refers to the perfecting of Christ by consecration to the priesthood it is stated: "both he that sanctifieth and they that are sanctified are all of one" or perhaps "he that sanctifieth and they that are sanctified form a complete whole" (2:11). If the perfecting of Christ consists in a priestly consecration, it is the same for the faithful because of the unity of Sanctifier and sanctified. The state of perfection therefore to which we are brought by the unique oblation of Christ is not primarily a moral or spiritual perfection but a priestly state of consecration. By His sacrifice Christ has made us a royal priesthood; He has consecrated us. And this consecration takes effect in us through baptism into His death, which is the very act of consecration of the faithful to the royal priesthood. All holiness and all moral and spiritual perfection spring from this. This consecration is a true perfecting in the sense that it is identical with the salvation offered to us by the sacrifice of Christ.

Nothing is subtracted from the value of the unique oblation of Christ by baptism into His death which confers individually the royal priesthood. Here is the true meaning of the uniqueness of the sacrifice of the cross. It is the source, the meaning and the unity of every action of the Church; it is the source, the meaning and the unity of every baptism, of every Eucharist, of every act of preaching, of every prayer.... And the sacrifice of the cross is this source, this meaning and this unity because it is a continual offering, and a unique historical event continued in the heavenly intercession of Christ until He come again.

It is to be noted that although, in Hebrews, sanctification is regarded as something already achieved from God's side, it is also something which is being achieved in its personal application to men. "We have been sanctified (past) through the offering of the body of Jesus Christ once for all" (10: 10); but yet "by one offering he hath perfected for

[1] Spicq, *op. cit.*, p. 222.

ever them that are sanctified (present)" (10: 14). The completeness of the sacrifice of Christ does not exclude a progression in the application of its fruits to men. And this application, which is the work of the Church the Body of Christ, by preaching, the sacraments and prayer, is sustained and borne before the face of God by Christ Himself, the heavenly High Priest and living intercessor. In this heavenly intercession He gathers together in the unity of a single great sacrifice His oblation on the cross and the whole work of the Church His Body which, through its ministry, makes present to each one the unique and perfect sacrifice of its Lord.

"Now where remission of sins is, there is no more offering for sin" (10: 18). In the sacrifices of the old covenant, there was a memorial of sins, a recalling to God and men of the condition of sin in which the whole of humanity finds itself (10: 3). In the oblation of the body of Jesus Christ there is remission of sins (10: 10, 18). The undoubted parallelism of ἀνάμνησις (memorial) and ἄφεσις (remission) emphasizes the objective character of these two realities. The Epistle to the Hebrews does not deny the objective value of the cultus of the old covenant, but it demonstrates its negative character; the repeated sacrifice is an objective memorial, a proclamation of sin, which brings an accusation against men; it is an everlasting confession. The offering of the body of Jesus Christ, unique and perfect, is a remission of sins which is complete and final.

It is important to note this parallelism between *memorial* and *remission* elsewhere in the New Testament, in the accounts of the institution of the Eucharist. In Matthew (26: 28) the saying over the cup is: "this is my blood of the covenant, which is shed for many unto remission of sins." And in 1 Corinthians 11: 25: "This cup is the new covenant in my blood: this do, as oft as ye drink it, for my memorial." The memorial of Christ and the remission of sins are thus placed in parallel. It is no longer a question of a memorial of sin, but of remission of sins. The Eucharist recalls the mercy of the Father by presenting sacramentally the unique oblation of the body of Christ upon the cross. Of course the remission of sins is the fruit of this unique oblation of the cross, but that oblation is presented and made present because of its presence before the Father through the heavenly intercession of the Son. If it were necessary to understand the uniqueness of the oblation of the body of Christ and of the remission of sins in the sense of an isolated act in past history without duration or extension, then the Epistle to the Hebrews would condemn every sacrament, every

11

application and actualization of the sacrifice of Christ and every confession of sins for the purpose of receiving absolution. But the New Testament does reveal elsewhere the preaching of repentance and baptism in water as acts issuing in the remission of sins (Mk. 1: 4; Lk. 3: 3; 24: 47; Acts 2: 38). "Thus it is written, that the Christ should suffer, and rise again from the dead the third day; and that repentance and remission of sins should be preached in his name unto all the nations, beginning from Jerusalem. . . . Repent ye, and be baptized every one of you in the name of Jesus Christ unto the remission of your sins; and ye shall receive the gift of the Holy Ghost" (Lk. 24: 46 f.; Acts 2: 38). By the memorial of Christ in the Eucharist, as by water baptism and the preaching of repentance, the remission of sins, obtained once for all for the people of God on the cross, is made present for each of those who welcome it in personal faith and in the faith of the Church.

The uniqueness of the oblation of Christ for the remission of sins cannot be over-emphasized; it is a fundamental theme in the Epistle to the Hebrews. It is indeed difficult to reconcile with this New Testament affirmation a certain conception of the mass as a repetition of the cross which is found in those Roman Catholic circles which are theologically unenlightened. Yet it should be remembered that the Epistle to the Hebrews was not written against the sacrifice of the mass; it has in view the worship of the old covenant. By denying any sacrificial interpretation of the Eucharist and by insisting on the uniqueness of the oblation of the cross for the remission of sins, in the sense of an action without duration or extension, certain Protestant circles have often lost faith in the present efficacy of the sacraments for the remission of sins and have retained only a symbolical remembrance of a past act. Is there not here an explanation also of the abandonment of confession and sacramental absolution by Protestants? To understand "once for all" in a purely historical sense, without taking into account the dimension provided by the heavenly intercession of Christ, is to destroy faith in the necessity of confession with a view to possible, present and effective remission of sins. The Epistle to the Hebrews needs to be considered again in an ecumenical perspective, without assimilating the Roman mass to the sacrifices of the Old Testament, in order to rediscover the vision of Christ, the heavenly intercessor, who presents before the Father His unique and perfect offering for sin on the cross and applies it to each believer in the Word and Sacraments of the Church.

"For by one offering he hath perfected for ever them that are sanctified" (10: 14). This perfecting in salvation and this consecration in the royal priesthood are secured to the people of God throughout the centuries. It is a work accomplished in time, once for all on the cross, which has a continual duration. This people, brought to salvation and consecrated, is composed of members who, even today, are sanctified by the sacrifice of the cross. This making present of the unique oblation of Christ is possible because the risen Lord has entered into glory in heaven "whither as a forerunner Jesus entered for us, having become a high priest for ever after the order of Melchizedek" (6: 20). Because of the living intercession of Christ in heaven, the oblation of the cross is continually present before the face of the Father and it continues to sanctify the consecrated members of the people of God by means of the Word and the Sacraments.

In this perspective the Eucharist can be called a sacrifice. It is not an independent sacrifice, having its efficacy in itself. It draws all its strength from the unique offering of Christ which it represents, presents and makes present. The Eucharist is a sacrifice in the sense that it is the presence of Christ crucified, glorified and interceding, of Him who presents now for us His unique sacrifice before the face of the Father. The Eucharist is a sacrifice because it is one with the heavenly intercession of Christ which is the continual extension of the sacrifice of the cross. The Eucharist presents to the Father the unique sacrifice of the Son on the cross, in union with the heavenly intercession of Christ. Thus there is a single offering of the body of Christ under three aspects:

(a) the unique and perfect sacrifice of Christ on the cross—this is an historical action and is the foundation of salvation.

(b) the heavenly and perpetual sacrifice of Christ in intercession—this is an eternal act which makes salvation present.

(c) the memorial and sacramental sacrifice of Christ in the Eucharist—this is a liturgical act comprising the sacrament of salvation.

The Eucharist is therefore a sacrifice in so far as it is the memorial and sacrament of the unique sacrifice of the cross and of the heavenly sacrifice of the intercession of Christ. It is the memorial of the sacrifice of Christ because it presents it before the Father as a living and present intercession; it is the sacrament of the sacrifice of Christ because it makes it present before the Church as an effective and actual means of sanctification. The Eucharist, as the memorial and sacrament of the sacrifice of Christ, is one with the cross and with the heavenly intercession of Christ. Cajetan clearly defined, for Roman Catholic theology, the meaning and the limits of the eucharistic sacrifice in

B

relation to the sacrifice of the cross: "It is not to be wondered at that every day the sacrifice of the altar is offered in the Church of Christ; because it is not a new sacrifice but the very same which Christ offered and of which the memorial is made, according to the command of Christ Himself: 'Do this in remembrance of me.' Every sacrament is no more than an application of the passion of Christ to those who receive it. Indeed it is one thing to repeat the passion of Christ and another to repeat the memorial and the application of the passion of Christ."[1]

The writer to the Hebrews considers the sacrifice of the Old Testament as a memorial of sin without the possibility of any true remission, but the Eucharist is the memorial and the sacrament of the remission of sins obtained once for all on the cross for the entire people of God.

Just as the sacrifices of the Old Testament recalled continually before God and men the sin from which the latter could never be set free, so the Eucharist of the new covenant, the memorial and the sacrament of the unique sacrifice of Christ, recalls sacramentally before God and men the remission of sins through the oblation of the body of Christ. Because of the sacrifice of Christ on the cross and of His heavenly intercession, the Father "remembers his mercy and his holy covenant" (Lk. 1: 54, 72), and He grants remission of sins to all those who repent and who believe, by means of the Word and the Sacraments, and pre-eminently by means of the sacrament of the sacrifice of Christ, the Eucharist, for the Lord Himself said: "This is my blood of the covenant, which is shed for many unto remission of sins" (Matt. 26: 28).

THE MEMORIAL OF PRAYER AND CHARITY

The second passage in the New Testament where the word memorial is to be found is in the tenth chapter of Acts, which recounts the vision of the Roman centurion Cornelius (10: 1-6). Cornelius, a centurion of the Italian cohort at Caesarea, is a pious man, a God-fearer, i.e. one who sympathizes with Judaism but has not yet become a member of the chosen people by circumcision: "he gave much alms to the people, and prayed to God alway" (10: 2). He has a vision in which the angel of God, who wishes to put him in touch with the apostle Peter, calls to him and reveals that this vision is an answer to his devotion: "Thy prayers and thine alms are gone up for a memorial before God" (10: 4). There is no trace in this of any sort of "Pelagianism" to the effect that God bestows His grace in response to an effort on the part of the natural man. Indeed, the centurion is not a pagan; as a God-fearer he is

[1] Quoted by Spicq, op. cit., p. 312.

already connected with the chosen people and with the Lord, by faith, devotion and obedience. He is a believer touched by the grace of God, although he is not yet institutionally incorporated into the chosen people. Both the vision and vocation of God therefore appear as a free gift of God to a man whose devotion is one with the faith of Israel. God gives a reward for what He has Himself bestowed. Nevertheless it must be emphasized, in opposition to a certain theological "quietism", that the angel does acknowledge the efficacy of the prayers and alms of Cornelius: there is a reward, a response to the faith, hope and charity, to the prayer and alms of a believer.

There is no doubt that this passage alludes to the memorial-oblation or *azkarah* which was an offering of flour, oil and incense (Lev. 2: 2, 9, 16; 5: 12; 6: 8 etc.). It has been shown, in Part I, that this memorial-oblation had become a symbol of prayer ascending before God and borne up by intercessory angels. This liturgical image is quite in place in this context. The angel who speaks to Cornelius is one of the numerous ministers of this heavenly intercession, by which the prayers of the saints are borne up before God like an offering of incense (Rev. 5: 8; 8: 3). It would appear that this liturgical image must have been current in religious language since a God-fearer could understand it. In any case an explanation is given of it later by Cornelius himself when he describes his vision to Peter. "The angel said to me: 'Cornelius, thy prayer is heard, and thine alms are had in remembrance in the sight of God'" (10: 31). Cornelius thus gives an exegesis of the memorial. The prayers and alms, symbolized by the memorial-oblation, are had in remembrance, recalled before God, by the intercessory angels. The memorial is a recalling to God, a supplication which ascends before Him that it may be granted. It is the same conception of the prayer-memorial, symbolized by a liturgical oblation, which we have noted at the opening of Ps. 141: 2:

> Let my prayer be set forth as incense before thee;
> The lifting up of my hands as the evening sacrifice.

The use of the passive—"are had in remembrance"—should not be regarded simply as a means of speaking respectfully about God. The form suggests the intervention of the angels. It does indeed emphasize the respect due to God who sits in the heavenly court, but it is no less objective because of this. So Matthew uses the passive or impersonal form in a context which relates to the intercessory role of the angels: "See that ye despise not one of these little ones; for I say unto you, that in heaven their angels do always behold the face of my Father which is in heaven. . . . Even so it is not the will of your Father which is in heaven, that one of these little ones should perish" (Matt. 18: 10, 14). Again there is the same vision of the face of God *before* which stand the intercessory angels, who present those prayers and alms of the faithful, as a memorial; they recall to Him, they bring to His remembrance, that He may hear. The memorial before God is here once more related to the ministry of the angels, and it is essentially a recalling to God and an intercession.

The book of Tobit provides an example of a situation similar to that of Cornelius. Raphael, speaking to Tobit and his son Tobias, says: "Good is prayer with fasting and alms and righteousness. A little with righteousness is better than much with unrighteousness. It is better to give alms than to lay up gold: alms doth deliver from death, and it shall purge away all sin. They that do alms and righteousness shall be filled with life; but they that sin are enemies to their own life. . . . And now, when thou didst pray, and Sarah thy daughter-in-law, I did bring the memorial of your prayer before the Holy One: and when thou didst bury the dead, I was with thee likewise" (12: 8–10, 12). Here, as in the vision of Cornelius, alms and prayer are associated and there is reference to a memorial carried up before God by an angel. Alms, a sign of charity, are effective like prayer; they are a memorial.

In Ecclesiasticus the same connexion between alms, as a sign of charity, and the liturgical memorial is made:

> He that requiteth a good turn offereth fine flour;
> And he that giveth alms sacrificeth a thank offering (35: 2).

In traditional spirituality the memorial-oblation had thus become a symbol of prayer and of charity, and alms, a sign of charity, were understood to be the equivalent of a liturgical sacrifice. Charity and liturgy were thus united in the same symbol of the memorial. Charity, like prayer, ascends as a memorial before God, like the liturgical oblation and like the thank offering.

Worship and charity were to be united in this same perspective in the New Testament and signs of charity were to be considered as thank offerings. The author of Hebrews writes: "Through him then let us offer up a sacrifice of praise to God continually, that is, the fruit of lips which make confession to his name. But to do good and to communicate forget not: for with such sacrifices God is well pleased" (13: 15 f.). The liturgical reference is clear. "Through him" at the beginning of the verse is parallel with "by the high priest" in verse 11. Christ is the High Priest, and through Him, by His intercession, we offer the sacrifice of praise or thanksgiving, which is the highest form of the Jewish cultus, the *zebach todah* (Lev. 7: 12; Pss. 50: 14; 116: 17); this sacrifice is the fruit of the lips (Hos. 14: 2, LXX), i.e. the proclamation of the Name of Christ. And the following verse adds that this sacrifice is also fraternal charity. Thus the whole of the Christian life is summed up in this image of the sacrifice of thanksgiving: faith, witness, worship, prayer, charity, obedience, all are unified in the unique sacrifice of the Church's praise which is received up through Christ, the heavenly High Priest.

The Church now enjoys that reality to which the Jewish tradition looked forward at the coming of the Messiah, when all acts of worship would be summed up in thanksgiving which alone would last for ever.[1]

St. Paul also considered mutual aid as "an odour of a sweet smell, a sacrifice acceptable, well-pleasing to God" (Phil. 4: 18). Thus, under the new covenant, charity, with its material signs, is fully united to prayer and worship and symbolized by the image of the sacrifice of thanksgiving. By the gift of his possessions, as a sign of charity, the Christian accomplishes a true sacrifice of thanksgiving, as when he confesses the name of Christ in worship, prayer or witness. The image of the sacrifice of thanksgiving unifies liturgy and charity, prayer and alms, in a single spiritual movement: the memorial which through the priesthood of Christ ascends before the Father to thank Him for all His benefits and to ask Him to remember, yet again and always, His people.

If the prayers and alms of Cornelius ascended as a memorial before God, does this mean that there is some merit in the good works of the faithful? The conception of merit is no more to be found in Cornelius's alms than in his prayers. His alms are identified with his prayers in the symbol of the memorial; his charity, revealed by the concrete sign of giving his goods, is a sacrifice of thanksgiving and a prayer, a means of thanking and invoking the Lord, not only in words but in action. There is no merit, in the usual sense, in the prayers and alms of Cornelius, but there is efficacy in this gift of himself to God in prayer and charity. God responds by hearing the sacrifice of praise and supplication which ascends from the heart of Cornelius as a memorial

---

[1] This was the belief of the rabbis Phineas (*c.* 360), Levi (*c.* 300) and Johannan (*c.* 279); Strack-Billerbeck, I, p. 246.

before Him.[1] But this sacrifice of thanksgiving and intercession was made possible only by the grace of God who had given to Cornelius both the desire to pray and the stimulus of his charity. In this instance, God, as always, rewards His own gifts. The symbol of the memorial-oblation assimilates the works of charity to the prayer of faith and rules out every notion of merit. Prayers and alms were the freely bestowed sacrifice of Cornelius to which God in His grace responded.

It is in connexion with the memorial that we may consider afresh the meaning of the eucharistic offertory. The gifts of the faithful, in money or in kind, may be related to the Eucharist within the context of the memorial. The community offers its alms to the Lord, as a memorial, as a prayer of thanksgiving and intercession, but at the same time it signifies, by this action, the brotherly love by which it lives. The offering of material goods to the Lord and the giving of them to the needy brethren are one and the same sacrifice: the memorial of the alms which ascends before God and then descends in blessing upon each one.

The role of the offertory in the Eucharist cannot be too much stressed. It provides a powerful means of integrating the whole life of the believers and their brotherly charity with the eucharistic celebration itself. The liturgy does not then appear as something separate and exclusive, without any direct connexion with life. On the contrary, the Eucharist becomes a privileged means of expressing brotherly charity and of self-giving in spiritual sacrifice. Eucharist and daily life are but one: the Eucharist allows life to be expressed under the form of praise, charity and sacrifice; daily life itself is brought into the Eucharist and provides it with "matter" to sanctify, to vivify and to bless for the welfare of all.

This offering of the Church is recalled in the eucharistic prayer itself, and charity is thus brought into close relationship with the unique sacrifice of Christ proclaimed in the prayer. Christ takes us as we are; He takes our offering, however poor it may be, in order to

[1] "The angel assigns this as the cause why God vouchsafes to show to Cornelius the light of His Gospel; because He has heard his prayers and accepted his alms. Whence we gather that virtues and good works do not only please God, but they are also adorned with this excellent reward, that heaps upon us and enriches us with greater gifts for their sake; according to that, 'To him that hath shall be given'." Calvin, *Commentary* on Acts 10: 4. It is noticeable that Calvin in no way minimizes this "reward" for alms. He adds: "For God does after this sort extol His own by a continual course of His gifts, as it were by certain steps, until He bring them to the top."

purify it and make it subservient to the glory of the Father and the welfare of our brethren. The conclusion of the eucharistic prayer emphasizes the presence of our spiritual sacrifice in the memorial of the sacrifice of Christ. In this magnificent conclusion not only is the spiritual sacrifice of the Church integrated with the sacrifice of Christ, but the Church's offering, its gifts and charity, is considered to have its origin in God. It is He that has created all things that we may offer them to Him by consecrating them to His glory and to the welfare of our brethren: ". . . through Christ our Lord; by whom, O Lord, Thou dost ever create, hallow, quicken, bless and bestow upon us all these good things. By Him, and with Him, and in Him, be unto Thee, O God the Father Almighty, in the unity of the Holy Spirit, all honour and glory, world without end. Amen."

This ending of the Roman eucharistic prayer is a faithful echo of David's prayer when he had gathered the materials to build the Temple: "Now therefore, our God, we thank thee, and praise thy glorious name. But who am I, and what is my people, that we should be able to offer so willingly after this sort? *for all things come of thee, and of thine own have we given thee*" (1 Chron. 29: 13 f.).

It is evident, in the vision of Cornelius analysed above, that the memorial of his prayers and alms is a sacrifice which ascends before God. It has been previously stated that the term *mnemosunon*, used in this passage, is the equivalent of *anamnesis*, used in the Lucan and Pauline passages relating to the Eucharist. This confirms once more the very rich meaning of the word memorial as it designates the eucharistic celebration. It may be likened to the oblation which ascends as a memorial before God. It is the memorial of the entire redemptive work of Christ presented to the Father in thanksgiving and intercession. It is received through the heavenly intercession of Christ the High Priest in the communion of the intercessory angels and of all the saints. The Eucharist is above all that unique sacrifice of thanksgiving or praise which alone can continue, according to the Jewish tradition, after the coming of the Messiah. It is the sacrifice of thanksgiving which expresses gratitude continually to the Lord for the wonderful works of redemption, in order that He may this day grant the benefit of this to all men in the forgiveness of sins. The fact that the Eucharist is a sacrifice of thanksgiving implies intercession for all men and prayer for the remission of their sins. But, because it makes present before the Father and before men the unique oblation of the body of Christ, since it is integrated with the perfect sacrifice of Christ on Calvary and with His living intercession in heaven, it is a peaceable sacrifice full of the assurance that it will be accepted.

THE MEMORIAL OF THE SAINTS

The word *mnemosunon* is also found in the parallel passages in Mark and Matthew which record the anointing at Bethany (Mk. 14: 9; Matt. 26: 13). Jesus is at table in the house of Simon the leper; a woman enters "having an alabaster cruse of ointment of spikenard very costly". She breaks the vessel and empties it upon His head. Some of those present are indignant as they think of the value of this precious perfume. The price could have been given to the poor, it could have been used for alms. But Jesus takes up her defence: "She hath wrought a good work on me." The poor are always there; good can be done to them whenever one wants, but Christ Himself is soon to leave the earth. "She hath done what she could: she hath anointed my body aforehand for the burying." Then the Lord provides this solemn ending to His words: "Verily I say unto you, Wheresoever the gospel shall be preached throughout the whole world, that also which this woman hath done shall be spoken of for a memorial of her."

At several points in this passage there is a reference to good works. Some of the guests think of alms that could have been given—an especially good work. Jesus declares that the woman's action is a good work and He explains this work as one of piety, namely that of a woman preparing a body for burial. What the woman has done is the equivalent of almsgiving and of burying the dead, two actions regarded as good works. One need only recall the alms of Cornelius which ascended as a memorial before God and the work of Tobit, in burying the dead, which was presented by the angel Raphael as a memorial before God. The woman, hereafter called Mary[1], made a gesture of love and adoration before Christ, and He ascribes to this the value of a good work, of alms or of burying the dead. This context demands, quite naturally, the use of the term memorial. Her gesture of piety is a true memorial before God, as were those of Tobit and Cornelius. Her costly offering ascends towards her Lord as a memorial, as a prayer or almsgiving or any other act of charity.

In view of the Jewish background to this term, the expression "for a memorial of her" cannot mean "in memory of her"; it does not refer to a simple act of remembrance, any more than Christ's "for my

---

[1] Neither Mark nor Matthew give her a name; John identifies her with Mary, the sister of Lazarus (12: 1–8).

memorial" at the Last Supper. This expression is to be interpreted within the context of the liturgical memorial, which was a symbol of the offering of self in prayer and in deed.[1] Like the offerings of Tobit and Cornelius, that of Mary is a memorial before God. Mary's gesture is an acted giving of praise which recalls her before the Lord; it is a memorial of her, and God will remember her. This memorial is not therefore just a remembrance by men who will recall her exemplary action, it is above all an act of praise which will ascend like the prayer of the saints presented to God by the angels: ". . . that which this woman hath done shall be spoken of . . ." It may be suggested that "shall be spoken of" refers to a proclamation by the angels as they transmit the praise of the saints to the Lord. Not only will the Church recall the action of Mary before God, but the angels in their turn will bear it before the Lord like incense (Rev. 5: 8; 8: 3). This passive form recalls the passage in Acts (10: 31) where the angelic court is evidently in mind: "Cornelius, thy prayer is heard, and thine alms are had in remembrance in the sight of God."

This allusion to the angelic memorial before God, which recalls to Him Mary's act of praise, is made even clearer if the passage is understood in an eschatological sense.[2] According to this interpretation, ὅπου ἐὰν has a temporal sense and not a spatial one; it should be translated "when" and not "wheresoever".[3] Further, "the gospel shall be preached throughout the whole world" may be related to the proclamation of the angel on the Day of Judgment. "And I saw another angel flying in mid heaven, having an eternal gospel to proclaim unto them that dwell on the earth, and unto every nation and tribe and tongue and people; and he saith with a great voice, Fear God, and give him glory; for the hour of his judgment is come; and worship him that made the heaven and the earth and sea and fountains of waters" (Rev. 14: 6 f.). This eternal gospel is the Word of God in creation, the perpetual promise of the love of God which will be proclaimed in the last times, before the Judgment, to invite all men to worship.[4] The

[1] J. Jeremias, *The Eucharistic Words of Jesus*, 1955, p. 163, considers this interpretation to be "highly probable". Cf. E. Lohmeyer, *Das Evangelium des Markus*, 1937, pp. 295 f., and J. Jeremias, "Mark 14: 9", *Z.N.W.*, XLIV, 1952, pp. 103-7.

[2] J. Jeremias, *ibid.*, understands Mk. 14: 9 in this eschatological sense.

[3] The Syriac *sys* understands ὅπου as a temporal conjunction (*kadh*); ὅπου ἐὰν in Mk. 9: 18 has also a temporal meaning: "whensoever it taketh him, it dasheth him down."

[4] C. Masson, "L'Evangile éternel de l'Apocalypse, 14: 6 et 7", *Hommage et reconnaissance à Karl Barth*, 1946, pp. 63-7.

reference to this solemn proclamation in the account of the anointing at Bethany would therefore relate the memorial of Mary to the Day of Judgment, and Jesus' saying would then mean: "When the Good News (eternal, on the last day) shall be proclaimed throughout the whole world (by the angel flying in mid heaven), that also which this woman has done shall be spoken of (borne before God) as a memorial of her (that the Lord may remember her in the Last Judgment)."[1]

It does not however appear that this eschatological interpretation of Jesus' saying concerning Mary can be maintained exclusively. In fact, the expression "to proclaim the gospel" has in Mark a present meaning also, designating the preaching of the Church (13: 10; 16: 15). It is therefore not possible to see here only the angelic proclamation on the Day of Judgment, just as it is not possible to exclude completely the eschatological interpretation. We must be content with a certain mystery in this saying which can embrace the proclamation both of the Kingdom by the Church and of the eternal gospel by the angel.

What must be noted is that the proclamation of the gospel, either present or final, is to be accompanied by the memorial of Mary. The gospel of the Kingdom preached by the Church and the eternal gospel declared by the angel are both to be accompanied by a recalling of what Mary has done, a recalling before God that He may remember. The proclamation of the Gospel of Christ does not exclude, indeed it includes, the recalling of the saints, of their faith, their hope and their charity. The title "saint" is used here in the New Testament sense of "a believer in Christ, incorporated into His Body and sanctified by His Spirit". Nevertheless it is evident that some of the faithful, like Mary, are by vocation detached from the mass of the communion of saints in order that they may be, by their witness, an example and a stimulus to the Church and a particular sign of the holiness common to all believers. Thus the whole Church is edified and built up by recalling the faith and life of a saint. Mary, by her gesture of adoration, sums up the whole company of the saints who have offered to God that which is most precious, without counting the cost, and have given their lives in complete consecration to the Lord. This recalling of the faith and obedience of the saints does not diminish the absolute honour that the Church owes to its unique Lord. The faith and life of the saints reflect the many aspects of the divine grace and are thus a new

---

[1] Cf. Jeremias, *op. cit.*, p. 163, n. 3: "Amen, I say unto you, when the news (of victory) will be proclaimed, what this (woman) has done will be reported (before God), that (He) may remember her (at the Last Judgment)."

act of praise to His glory alone. The recalling of the saints in the Church's liturgy is a theological necessity, for they are themselves a recalling of the mediation of Christ in His Church universal throughout the ages. The Son of God, in His incarnation, wished to be present to men through the mediation of His humanity. When He had risen, He wished to leave signs that would recall and make present this mediation: the combination of these signs is the Church, the Body of Christ. Each member is a sign of the presence of the Lord, and God desires us to meet Him in the faith, hope and charity of our brethren. The saints are therefore signs of the presence and love of Christ. Through them Christ has shown forth His presence and love in our humanity. To forget them or to ignore them is to interrupt the continuity of the Church. To omit to recall the saints in the liturgy impoverishes our sense of tradition, of the continuity of Christ's presence in the Church, and of the faithfulness of God throughout history. The recalling of the saints together with the proclamation of the good news is a sign of the continuity of the Church and of the faithfulness of God, and it is a theological necessity that faith in the unity of the Body of Christ and in the communion of the saints may be maintained.[1]

This presence of Mary of Bethany and of the saints in association with the proclamation of the gospel is not simply a recalling to mind; it is, as Christ Himself stated, a memorial of her, in the full sense of the term. Her unique action, recalled with the gospel, is presented to God as a memorial that He may remember her. According to the eschatological interpretation, her action will be a defence for her at the Last Judgment, in the same way that every act of charity will equally be a defence for each one of us: to give food to the hungry, drink to the thirsty, to welcome the stranger, to clothe the poor, to visit the sick and the prisoners (Matt. 25: 35–40). But we have preferred a wider interpretation of the passage. There will be a final memorial of Mary at the final proclamation of the eternal gospel by the angel, as there will be a final memorial on our behalf at the Last Judgment, when Christ recalls our acts of mercy towards "one of these my brethren, even these least" (Matt. 25: 40), that is to say, unto Him. But there is also today, with the present proclamation of the gospel of the Kingdom by the Church, a memorial of Mary of Bethany, of her adoration and charity, a memorial of all the saints, of their faith and life, before the Lord. This memorial is accomplished in the

[1] M. Thurian, "Marie dans la Bible et dans l'Eglise", *Dialogue sur la Vièrge*, 1950, pp. 123–5; "Le dogme de l'assomption", *Verbum Caro*, 17, 1951, pp. 36 f.

23

heavenly liturgy of the angels who offer the prayers of all the saints like incense "upon the golden altar which was before the throne" (Rev. 8: 3).

If, on Judgment Day, this memorial will be presented on Mary's behalf, and if today it remains present within the heart of Christ, it is evident that the Church cannot present it to God as an intercession for Mary. Because of the communion of saints and the mutual intercession of believers, the memorial on behalf of Mary becomes, within the Body of Christ, a memorial on behalf of all the faithful. That is why, in the early Church, prayer *for* the apostles, prophets and martyrs, becomes after their death prayer *with* them, in the communion of saints, on behalf of the whole Church. In many early prayers "to pray for" the saints frequently means to be united to the prayer of the saints, to unite their faith and their prayer to the worship of the Church. Some prayers make this meaning explicit by using the formula "to make remembrance of", in the sense of the memorial of their existence and prayer before God. This reference to the saints in the liturgy reveals the unity of the Church throughout the ages and the brotherhood of the communion of saints in mutual intercession. The prayer in the *Apostolic Constitutions*, a fourth-century document of Syrian provenance, reads:

> We further offer to Thee also for all those saints who have pleased Thee from the beginning of the world—patriarchs, prophets, righteous men, apostles, martyrs, confessors, bishops, presbyters, deacons, subdeacons, readers, singers, virgins, widows, and lay persons, with all whose names Thou knowest. We further offer to Thee for this people, that Thou wilt render them, to the praise of Thy Christ, a royal priesthood and an holy nation.[1]

It is evident that "we further offer to Thee for" has not exactly the same sense in each case. In the first, the reference is to a memorial of the saints, in the second to a prayer for the Church militant. But in both cases there is reference to a communion in prayer, to a gathering together of the whole Church in the liturgy. The same is true of the litany in the *Testamentum Domini*, edited in the fifth century but from sources which are much older:

> Let us pray for patience; that the Lord will grant us patience in all our trials, unto the end.
> Let us pray for the apostles; that the Lord will grant us to please Him, as they have pleased Him, and that He may make us worthy of their inheritance.

[1] 8: 12.

Let us pray for the holy prophets; that the Lord may count us among them.

Let us pray for the holy confessors; that the Lord may grant us to finish our lives in the same spirit.

Let us pray for the bishop; that the Lord may preserve him long in the faith.[1]

The formula "let us pray for", in this passage, has three meanings: to pray for peace, faith, unity or patience, is to pray for the bestowal of these gifts; to pray for the apostles, prophets or confessors is to make the memorial of them, to ask to partake of the gifts they have received, to be "made worthy of their inheritance"; to pray for the bishop, priests, deacons, etc. is to intercede for them, to ask on their behalf for the graces they need for their life and ministry in the Church.

Other prayers make this difference explicit by using "Lord, we pray Thee" for prayers on behalf of the Church or the world and "we make remembrance" for the memorial of the saints.[2]

The memorial of the saints in the early Church is clearly expressed in the litany of the Stowe Missal, which is a ninth-century Celtic edition of the primitive Roman rite:

Let us be mindful of the holy apostles and martyrs, that by their prayers for us, we may gain pardon.

There is then to be noted a movement from intercession for the faithful on earth to the memorial for the faithful departed, and these two types of prayer have a common denominator: the gathering together of the whole Church in the liturgy—the Church on earth and the Church in heaven.

The action of Mary of Bethany has provided the Church with a memorial. The Church has not to pray for Mary but prays with Mary, as with all the saints. It presents, in its prayer, the memorial of Mary to the Lord. It recalls before the Lord the faith, life and prayer of Mary, as of all the saints. It presents to the Lord this faith, this life, this prayer as its own, for Mary is a member of the Body of Christ. And the memorial of Mary, like the memorial of all the saints, becomes a prayer which is united to that of the Church in the Holy Spirit and to that of the angels, and is comprehended and borne up in the heavenly intercession of Christ ascending towards the Father of all mercies.

[1] 1: 35.
[2] See for example the deacon's litany in the Liturgy of St. James.

Each member of the Body of Christ, be he alive or dead, thus takes his place in the great prayer of the Church which, in the communion of the Holy Spirit and united to the adoration of the angels, offers to the Father its thanksgivings and intercessions through the mediation of the Son, its heavenly High Priest.

It is within the context of the memorial that the beatitude in Revelation 14: 13 is to be understood: "Blessed are the dead which die in the Lord from henceforth: yea, saith the Spirit, that they may rest from their labours; for their works follow with them." The works of the faithful departed are their faith and charity which accompany them and ascend to God as a final and confident prayer. Their works are a prayer-memorial that will enable them to enter into rest in expectation of the Last Judgment when their works-memorial will allow them to stand at the right hand of the Lord in the eternal Kingdom (Matt. 25: 34-40). But these works, although they are a kind of prayer-memorial before God, are effective only in so far as they are signs of faith and charity; they are not meritorious in themselves. The image of works accompanying the faithful at his death is also found in Judaism. According to Rabbi Jose ben Gisma (A.D. 90-130): "At the hour of his death, man is not accompanied by silver or gold or precious stones or pearls, but only by the Torah and *good works*."[1] It is however clear that, for the Jews, works go before the believer and become a criterion of judgment.[2] According to the commentaries on Deuteronomy: "When man is cut off from this age, his actions, all his actions, each one of them, go before him and he (God) says to him: You have acted thus on such a day and you have not believed these words. And he replies to him: Yes, yes. And he answers: It is sealed (Job 37: 7) . . . and he justifies his judgment."[3] The connexion between this rabbinic text and the image of the Last Judgment in Matthew (25: 31-46) is quite clear; but there is an essential difference. It is after having separated "the sheep from the goats" and placed the former "on his right hand" that the King shall say "unto them on his right hand, Come, ye blessed of my Father, inherit the kingdom prepared for you from the foundation of the world"; it is only then that He takes account of the good works of the faithful.

In the gospel then the order is the following: the separation of the righteous; the placing on the right hand of the King; their inheritance

[1] *Pirke Aboth*, 6: 9.
[2] E. Lohmeyer, *Die Offenbarung des Johannes*, 1953, p. 126.
[3] *Midrash Sifre on Deuteronomy*, 32: 4.

of the Kingdom and finally the recalling of their good works as signs of their faith and charity. The rabbinic order is different: the works go before the faithful departed; God recalls these works; the believer recognizes them and subscribes to the justice of the sentence. Hence according to the Tractate *Taanith*: "When man dies all his actions go before him; and it is said to him: is it thus that you acted in such a place on such a day? He replies: Yes, and he is told to subscribe (Job 37: 7; Ps. 51: 6). He subscribes and acknowledges the justice of his sentence."[1] In the same Talmud, in the Tractate *Aboda zara*, the opinion of Rabbi Jonathan (190–220) is recorded: "Every good action which a man performs in this world goes before him into the world to come, in accordance with what is written: Thy righteousness will go before thee (Is. 58: 8)."[2] If, in Judaistic thought, works precede the faithful departed like a cortège compounded of merit, according to the gospel God welcomes good works as an objectivization of the inner life, as a sign of faith and charity: they are an integral part of the Christian personality.[3]

The memorial of good works before God, like the action of Mary, is then a memorial of faith and charity, a memorial of the Christian entirely consecrated to his Lord: it is like a confident prayer fully assured of being heard. The works which accompany, or closely follow, the faithful departed (Rev. 14: 13) are a memorial of the faith, charity and consecration of their whole being and therefore a prayer that ascends before the Lord as a sign of love and praise. The opposition between salvation by faith and salvation by works has no longer any meaning when faith and works are considered in the unity of the consecration and adoration offered to the Lord as a memorial.

In the light of what has been said above, the memorial of Mary will now be more understandable. Her action of love and adoration is a good work which ascends before God as a memorial. This memorial is first of all a confident prayer on her behalf, and this memorial will be presented on her behalf at the Last Judgment. When the Church recalls this memorial, at the proclamation of the gospel, it recalls Mary's action before God. This is the occasion for the Church to associate itself with Mary's prayer, as with the prayer of all the saints,

[1] *Talmud babylonien, Ta'anit*, ed. Bonsirven, 1026, p. 258.
[2] *Ibid., Aboda zara*, 1998, p. 548.
[3] G. Bruetsch, *Clarté de l'Apocalypse*, 1955, p. 159: "Acts of faith directed towards one's neighbour are an integral part of the Christian's personal being."

27

in the unity of the Body of Christ. This memorial-prayer, which is first of all on behalf of the saints, does not remain an individual prayer for the benefit of a single person, but, within the communion of the Body of Christ, this memorial becomes that of the whole Church for the whole Church. Hence, when the Church recalls before God the memorial of Mary of Bethany, as that of all the saints, it presents to the Lord what Mary has done, her consecration and adoration, which remains as a permanent prayer, and it unites this prayer to its own intercession in the present for all mankind. The memorial of Mary and of all the saints, their consecration of faith, charity, works and prayer, is then like an intercession, which the Church offers with its own, as its own, because of the communion of the Body of Christ.

The commemoration of the saints in the liturgy is not then primarily or only a remembering to stimulate the faithful by their example, it is rather a communion in the same act of praise and in the same intercession of the departed saints, whose memorial of faith, charity, works and prayer, subsists before God, and of the Church which presents this memorial with its own prayer. It is of course to be admitted that by recalling the memorial of the saints the Church is primarily celebrating the divine grace in their lives and is trusting in that grace that God may abundantly grant it again in the present. The Church can then express itself thus in prayer:

> Remember, O Lord, Mary of Bethany and the adoration she offered to Thee; her praise is ours; it is by Thy grace that she grew and loved, acted and prayed; grant unto us, as unto her, the abundance of Thy grace that, in the communion of all the saints, and upheld by their prayer, we may persevere unto the end with them to the glory of Thy Kingdom, through Jesus Christ, Thy Son, our Lord, who liveth and reigneth with Thee, in the unity of the Holy Spirit, world without end. Amen.

The memorial of the saints finds its most appropriate place at the very point in the Eucharist where the Church presents *the* memorial of Christ. It is in Christ, and therefore within the eucharistic memorial of Christ, that the memorial of the saints, united to the prayer of the Church, ascends as an act of adoration and intercession towards the Father. In isolation, the memorial of the saints can become an illegitimate worship of the saints, where Christ is relegated to the background and His place taken by some individual or hero. But within the context of the eucharistic memorial of Christ, the memorial of the saints, far from detracting from the glory of the Lord, throws it into greater relief and emphasizes the powerful efficacy of the life, faith and prayer of all those who are consecrated to Him.[1]

The word "remember", so frequently used in the Old Testament, is also to be understood in the light of the memorial of the saints. The Lord is frequently besought to remember a patriarch, i.e. a saint of the old covenant, that He may renew His mercy. Obviously there is no question of recalling the individual merit of a saint, but the grace that was accorded him and which the Lord is asked to renew, e.g. the covenant with a patriarch. Nevertheless, it is the recalling of the covenant of God with a particular person, whose response to the divine vocation constitutes a memorial that may be presented before God. So, after the apostasy of the golden calf, Moses appeases Yahweh by praying: "Remember Abraham, Isaac, and Israel, thy servants, to whom thou swearest by thine own self, and saidst unto them, I will multiply your seed as the stars of heaven" (Ex. 32: 13). Moses also describes the incident thus: "And I prayed unto the Lord, and said, O Lord God, destroy not thy people and thine inheritance, which thou hast redeemed through thy greatness, which thou hast brought forth out of Egypt with a mighty hand. Remember thy servants, Abraham, Isaac, and Jacob; look not unto the stubbornness of this people, nor to their wickedness, nor to their sin . . . they are thy people and thine inheritance, which thou broughtest out by thy great power and by thy stretched out arm" (Deut. 9: 26–29). And the prayer of Solomon at the dedication of the Temple ends thus: "O Lord God, turn not away the face of thine anointed: remember the mercies of David thy servant" (2 Chron. 6: 42). In Ps. 132, which recalls the promise of the Messiah to David in answer to his oath to build a Temple for Yahweh, the anniversary of the translation of the ark was celebrated, beginning with these words:

> Lord, remember for David
> All his affliction.

This memorial of the holy patriarchs reveals the faithfulness of God and the continuity of His operation. It is always the same grace that

---

[1] The memorial of the saints can of course have a place in the office, outside the Eucharist, although its best place is within the latter, associated with the memorial of the cross and of the heavenly intercession. However, the office is not really independent from the Eucharist which it extends and for which it acts as a preparation. This connexion is made evident by the lections and special collects which remain the same for all celebrations, whether eucharistic or not, for the same feast.

He accords to His people by means of all those whom He calls. When Israel asks for the Messiah, it presents David to God, his faith and oath and the promise he received in return, and, strengthened by this memorial, it can ask for the messianic blessing.

Similarly the Church, when it celebrates the Eucharist, presents to the Father "the death of the Lord, until He come"; that is its most fervent supplication for the return of the Messiah: "Come Lord, *Maranatha!*" When it presents the Body of Christ, it includes within it all the members of that Body, all the saints who have lived and died in the hope of that return of Christ promised to them. When we make the memorial of Christ, as a supplication that He may return, we are making the memorial of all the saints, members of His Body, and we are presenting their faith, their hope and their charity as a prayer which pleads for the Lord's return. This memorial of the saints, contained in the memorial of Christ, signifies the unity of the Body of Christ and the continuity of its hope. The whole Church, advancing towards the Kingdom, implores the Lord to return.

The meaning of the memorial of the saints within the Eucharist may be summed up in some such simple prayer as this:

> Almighty and merciful God, remember the unique and perfect sacrifice of Thy Son, His Body the Church and each of its members in their several ministries; sanctify the faithful, accept the memorial of the saints because of their faith and their life; accept their intercession, through Jesus Christ, Thy Son, our Lord and God, who liveth and reigneth with Thee, in the unity of the Holy Spirit, world without end.[1]

"MAKING REMEMBRANCE"[2]

Before we go on to consider the accounts of the institution of the Eucharist, we must examine the word μνεία (*mneia*) in order to complete the survey of the use of the term memorial in the New Testament. Μνεία may be translated as "remembrance" or "re-

---

[1] On the memorial of the saints in Anglicanism see *The Commemoration of Saints and Heroes of the Faith in the Anglican Communion* (Report of Archbishop's Commission), 1957. On the history of the veneration of Mary in German Protestantism since the Reformation see R. Schimmelpfenning, *Die Geschichte der Marienverehrung im deutschen Protestantismus*, 1952. In French: *Dialogue sur la Vièrge*, 1950, and my contribution pp. 107-30, "Marie dans la Bible et dans l'Eglise". A supplement on the problem of the memorial of the saints has been published in *Verbum Caro*, XIII, 1959, No. 49.

[2] [French: *Faire mémoire.*]

collection",[1] and it has a somewhat subjective sense, although it cannot be entirely separated from the objective memorial. It is used only in the Pauline Epistles and in six of the seven passages it is connected with prayer. Further, in four instances, it is accompanied by the verb "to make" (poieo) and means "to make remembrance of someone" (Rom. 1: 9; Eph. 1: 16; 1 Thess. 1: 2; Philem. 4). Finally, in five passages, this "remembrance" is made by the apostle within the context of thanksgiving (eucharisteo, Eph. 1: 16; Phil. 1: 3; 1 Thess. 1: 2; 2 Tim. 1: 3). The passages are worth quoting in order to bring out their similarity: "How unceasingly I make mention (remembrance) of you, always in my prayers making request . . ." (Rom. 1: 9, 10); "I cease not to give thanks for you, making mention (remembrance) of you in my prayers . . ." (Eph. 1: 16); "I thank my God upon all my remembrance of you, always in every supplication of mine on behalf of you all making my supplication with joy . . ." (Phil. 1: 3 f.); "we give thanks to God always for you all, making mention (remembrance) of you in our prayers; remembering without ceasing your work of faith and labour of love and patience of hope in our Lord Jesus Christ . . ." (1 Thess. 1: 2 f.); "I thank God . . . how unceasing is my remembrance of thee in my supplications, night and day . . ." (2 Tim. 1: 3); "I thank my God always, making mention (remembrance) of thee in my prayers, hearing of thy love, and of the faith which thou hast toward the Lord Jesus, and toward all the saints . . ." (Philem. 4 f.). In all these passages "remembrance" is conceived to be an act of prayer before God and in particular a thanksgiving. In all instances St. Paul "makes remembrance" of the faithful before God in his prayer or thanksgiving. The word "remembrance" therefore in these passages has not just the subjective sense of "recollection", it does signify an objective action consisting of placing in prayer before God the remembrance of those for whom one prays and gives thanks. This is close to the idea of the memorial, mneia being a derivative which has preserved a quasi-liturgical meaning, for "remembrance" in the prayers of St. Paul is a recollection which becomes a memorial before God.

The passage which most brings out the connexion between memorial and remembrance is 1 Thessalonians 1: 2, 3. St. Paul, Silvanus and Timothy give thanks for the church of the Thessalonians. They make

[1] [The R.V. translates it by "mention" in four of the passages and by "remembrance" in the other three. In reproducing the biblical quotations I have adhered to the R.V. but added "remembrance" in brackets to show that this is what the author understands by the Greek original. Tr.]

remembrance of this church in their prayers. This remembrance becomes a memorial since it consists in recalling, before God the Father, the faith, charity and hope of the Thessalonians that they may thank Him for them. The activity, labour and constancy of this church become the content of the memorial of the apostles before God; they form the content of their prayer of thanksgiving. But if this "work" can be presented in a prayer of thanksgiving before God, it is not because it has a value or a merit of its own. It is the work of Christ Himself in the church at Thessalonica or the work of the Thessalonians in Christ, and this can be a legitimate and acceptable offering in thanksgiving to God.[1]

It is in this way that "to make remembrance of someone before God" is to be connected with the memorial. This is the most adequate expression of Christian prayer which, in its simplest form, is essentially a "remembrance before God" in order to "recall to God" all mankind. The purest Christian prayer is simply: "*Memento, Domine, famulorum famularumque tuarum* . . . Remember, O Lord, Thy servants and handmaidens."[2] It consists in remembering and making remembrance before God in prayer of those for whom intercession is offered that they may be recalled to the love of the Father by the intercession of Christ, in the communion of the Holy Spirit, that God may remember His covenant and mercy, and because of His blessings upon all the saints He may now bless those brought to Him in the memorial.

Reference should also be made to the robber's prayer to Jesus on the cross. It is an elementary and primitive form of the *memento:* "Jesus, remember me when thou comest in thy kingdom." And Jesus answered him: "Verily I say unto thee, Today shalt thou be with me in Paradise" (Lk. 23: 42 f.). The prayer, uttered at the point of death, is confined to what is the most essential and the most simple. It makes its appeal to the remembrance of God at the decisive moment when He will come to manifest His Kingdom. The eschatological character of this prayer recalls the eschatological interpretation of Mary's memorial at Bethany: God will remember her at the last day because of her act of charity. But although the robber's prayer looks forward

---

[1] It is to be noted that prayer, according to the Bible, consists first of all in praising God for the wonderful works He has accomplished and, within this act of praise, in asking Him to renew His blessings. See J. P. Audet, "Esquisse historique du genre littéraire de la bénédiction juive et de l'eucharistie chrétienne", *Revue Biblique*, LXV, 1958, pp. 371–99.

[2] This is the *Memento* of the living in the Roman rite.

to the Kingdom, Christ, in granting it, has the present in mind and foresees no delay. Jesus will remember the robber when He manifests His Kingdom at the last day, but already His hearing of the prayer bears its fruits: the robber from then on will be with Christ in Paradise, where he may await the Kingdom in peaceful expectation. A similar situation has been noted in connexion with Mary: the memorial of her charity will be presented on her behalf at the last day, but from today, when the Church proclaims the gospel, it associates itself with the heavenly court to speak of Mary of Bethany, as of all the saints, and to present to the Father her memorial, in the intercession of Christ and the communion of the Holy Spirit.

The *Didache* formulates a prayer for the unity of the Church in the Kingdom in these words: "Remember, O Lord, Thy Church, to deliver her from all evil, and to perfect her in Thy love, and gather together from the four winds her that is sanctified into Thy Kingdom which Thou didst prepare for her."[1] This same form of prayer, inspired by the memorial, is also found in the letters of Ignatius of Antioch: "Remember me, even as I would that Jesus Christ may also remember you. Pray for the Church which is in Syria, whence I am led a prisoner to Rome."[2] For Christians "to remember" or "to make remembrance" is the equivalent of "to pray", and, for God, it is the equivalent of "to hear, to grant, to show mercy".

[1] 10: 5.
[2] *Ad Eph.* 21.

II

THE WORDS OF CHRIST AT THE LAST SUPPER

HAVING PASSED UNDER review the biblical meaning of the memorial, we must now consider the accounts in the Gospels and by St. Paul which record the words of Christ when He instituted the Eucharist, which is the great memorial of the Lord.

First of all we shall consider the command of Christ to His apostles that His Church should celebrate the Eucharist until His return. Indeed, this command or liturgical rubric defines the meaning of the Eucharist and leads to an interpretation of the actions and words of Jesus over the bread and the cup. Certainly Christ's command is to be understood in the light of the biblical meaning of the memorial: "τοῦτο ποιεῖτε εἰς τὴν ἐμὴν ἀνάμνησιν, Do this as the memorial of me." This command is found once in Luke (22: 19b) and twice in St. Paul (1 Cor. 11: 24b, 25b). One point may be established at the outset and that is that the possessive "my" is the equivalent of an objective genitive: "of me",[1] as already noted in the account of the anointing at Bethany (Mk. 14: 9; Matt. 26: 13: "as a memorial of her").

THE ANAMNESIS OF THE MYSTERIES

That which the Lord commands the disciples "to do", the liturgy which He enjoins upon them, is designated by "this". It is clear that "this" relates to the whole of the eucharistic action: taking bread, giving thanks, breaking it, giving it, saying: "Take, eat; this is my body given for you"; taking the cup, giving thanks, giving it, saying: "Drink ye all of this; this is my blood (this cup is the new covenant in my blood) shed for you, for many, for the remission of sins." Justin Martyr, copying the account, fully understood that the command "to do this" related to the eucharistic action, since he transposed the order of the phrases: "Jesus took bread, and when He had given thanks, said, Do this as the memorial of me, this is my body."[2] In the Reformed Churches all the emphasis has been placed upon com-

[1] Jeremias, *op. cit.*, p. 162.
[2] *Apol.*, 1: 66.

34

munion, as if Christ's command referred only to "giving, taking, eating and drinking". Consequently the liturgy seems to be no more than an accompaniment, more or less important, more or less useful, to the essential action which is to communicate after having at least repeated the Lord's words. In Catholicism the reverse is to be noted; for reasons that need not be considered here, the communion of the faithful has become more or less optional at the mass, at which weekly attendance is an ecclesiastical rule. The whole accent is thus placed upon the celebration, as if Christ's command referred particularly to the reproduction of His actions and words: "Take the bread and the cup (Offertory), give thanks (Eucharistic Prayer), say: This is my body, this is my blood (Consecration), break the bread (Fraction)." The command to "take, eat and drink" thus concerns the priest and only secondarily and occasionally the faithful.[1] Communion at the mass thus appears to be no more than an optional adjunct which is not necessary, since what is essential is attendance at mass when the priest communicates.

Fortunately the liturgical renewal has led to a fuller understanding of and obedience to Christ's command: "Do this . . ." It has led to a rediscovery of the unity between the liturgy and the communion. Christ's command includes an entire sequence: offertory, eucharistic prayer, the words of institution, the fraction, the communion in both kinds of the ministers and the faithful. The liturgy of the Word (lections, psalms, prayers) quite naturally precedes this eucharistic liturgy, since the Lord comes to us with His Word and with His Body, in the Bible read and preached and in the Sacrament celebrated and communicated. "To do this" is therefore to execute a eucharistic *action*, a *giving* of thanks, a liturgical *celebration*, by word and deed.

This command to execute a eucharistic action is to be understood in the light of the words which by now are so full of meaning for us: "with a view to my memorial, in memorial of me, as the memorial of me." This memorial is not a simple subjective act of recollection, it is a liturgical action. But it is not just a liturgical action which makes the Lord present, it is a liturgical action which recalls as a memorial before the Father the unique sacrifice of the Son, and this makes Him present in His memorial, in the presentation of His sacrifice before the Father and in His intercession as heavenly High Priest. The eucharistic memorial is a recalling to us, a recalling by us to the Father and a

---

[1] In Western Catholicism, the faithful do not even have to observe the command to "drink ye all"—this is something of an anomaly.

recalling of the Son to the Father for us. Hence the eucharistic memorial is a proclamation by the Church; it is a thanksgiving and intercession of the Church and a thanksgiving and intercession of Christ for the Church.

When it celebrates the Eucharist, the Church places on the altar the signs of the sacrifice of Christ, the bread and the wine, His Body and His Blood, as Israel placed the shewbread on the golden table as a memorial before Yahweh. The Church, when it proclaims Christ's sacrifice, accomplishes on the altar the *shewing*-forth of the sacrifice of the Son before the Father, by thanksgiving and intercession, by praising Him and praying to Him. Thus the Church takes part in this action of shewing-forth the cross; it shares in the shewing-forth of the Lamb as it had been slain upon the heavenly altar and in that shewing-forth of His sacrifice which the Son performs before the Father, in thanksgiving and intercession.

When it performs this "shewing-forth" of the sacrifice of the cross, in union with the shewing-forth by the Son before the Father, the Church makes the memorial of the entire redemptive work of Christ; it gives thanks for all He has done for us and it intercedes with the Father that He may bestow upon mankind the blessings that have been obtained by the Son through all He has accomplished. This thanksgiving and intercession in terms of the memorial are constituted by the very act of celebration and not merely by the prayers that define its meaning. By reproducing the actions of Jesus at the Last Supper, the Church accomplishes the memorial of thanksgiving and intercession. The thanksgiving and intercession are not expressed by the words alone but by the whole of the eucharistic action, i.e. the actions of Christ with the signs of Christ, the bread and wine placed upon the altar—"the bread which we break and the cup of blessing which we bless" (1 Cor. 10: 16).[1]

By means of the prayers the Church makes explicit the action which is itself the memorial of thanksgiving and intercession; it declares what it is doing. It is in this way that the *anamnesis*, which makes explicit the meaning of the memorial in all liturgies, is to be understood. In the Roman rite this prayer follows the institution narrative:

Wherefore, O Lord, we Thy servants and likewise Thy holy people, mindful [*memores*, making the memorial] of the blessed passion of the same Thy Son our Lord Jesus Christ, and also His resurrection from the dead, and

---

[1] "The cup of blessing which we bless" i.e. "over which we pronounce the blessing of Christ" or "for which we give thanks".

His glorious ascension into heaven, offer unto Thy most excellent Majesty a pure host, a holy host, a spotless host, holy bread of eternal life, and the cup of everlasting salvation, which have been taken from the gifts Thou hast bestowed upon us [de tuis donis ac datis].[1]

The Eastern liturgies include other aspects of the total mystery of Christ: the cross and the tomb, the session at the right hand of the Father and the second coming (St. James, St. Basil, St. Chrysostom). Some East-Syrian anamneses add further mysteries: the conception, birth, baptism, passion, death, burial, resurrection, ascension, session at the right hand, return and judgment. The nativity also finds a place in the West at the end of the Carolingian period,[2] and the incarnation receives a mention in the Middle Ages.[3] Yet, whatever the number of the separate events in the life of Christ that are recalled, the anamnesis refers to the complete mystery of Christ.

The anamnesis of the liturgy of the Reformed Church of France may also be cited:

Holy and righteous Father, commemorating here the unique and perfect sacrifice, offered once for all on the cross by our Lord Jesus Christ, in the joy of His resurrection and in expectation of His coming, we offer ourselves to Thee as a living and holy sacrifice.[4]

And that of the liturgy of the Bernese Jura:

Remembering therefore, holy and righteous Father, the life and work of Thy beloved Son, His passion and death on the cross, His resurrection and His ascension to Thy right hand, confident in the promise of His return, we await the day when He will come in His power and glory. And awaiting His glorious coming, we now fulfil His commandment: we set forth, O God, in the presence of Thy divine Majesty, this bread and this wine which we have received from Thee, we give thanks to Thee for the redemptive work accomplished by Thy Son, and we bless Thee for the sacrifice that He has made of His body and blood, once for all on the cross. In communion with Thy Christ, our High Priest and Intercessor, we present to Thee, O God, our sacrifice of praise and the veneration of our hearts, and we consecrate wholly ourselves and our goods to Thy service in a living and holy offering.[5]

---

[1] The *Unde et memores*. The parenthetical clause, *de tuis donis ac datis*, is transferred in this quotation to the end that it may be referred to the bread and the wine.

[2] Bernold of Saint Blaise, *Micrologus* XIII (*P.L.* 151.985C), was opposed to this practice.

[3] The eleventh century Missal of Lagny.

[4] *Liturgie*, Eglise Reformée de France, 1955, p. 39.

[5] *Liturgie pour les paroisses de langue française*, I: Le culte, Eglise Reformée du Canton de Berne, 1955, p. 120. An alternative form, of Lutheran origin, is printed

Thus the eucharistic liturgy sets forth before the Father all that the Son has accomplished, from His conception in Mary to His entry into the heavenly sanctuary; sometimes it also makes the memorial of His return and of the Last Judgment, since these are promised in the Word of God. This latter, quite obvious, anachronism helps towards a deeper understanding of what the liturgy intends by the anamnesis: it is to plunge us into the total mystery of Christ which becomes present through the Eucharist.

A kind of telescoping of the successive events of the mystery of Christ is produced and this is presented to the Father in thanksgiving for what He has done and will do; it is offered as an intercession that all the fruits of this mystery may be given to the world now, and above all the fruit of the return of Christ and of the manifestation of the Kingdom.

Although, as has been noted, other events can be included in the anamnesis, the three essential foci are the passion, resurrection and ascension. Indeed the Eucharist appeals for the fruits of the death of Christ, of His resurrection and of His heavenly intercession, and this is summed up by St. Matthew in a single phrase: the remission of sins (26: 28b). The remission of sins is forgiveness through the passion of Christ; it is a renewing because of His resurrection and a setting free and a blessing because of His ascension: "When he ascended on high, he led captivity captive, and gave gifts unto men" (Eph. 4: 8).

The anamnesis has its special place in the eucharistic prayer after the words of institution, but the memorial must not be restricted to this alone. Indeed the whole eucharistic prayer is a memorial. Beginning with the preface, the mysteries of salvation are proclaimed before the Father in thanksgiving and intercession.[1] In the Eastern liturgies there

on p. 126. "Remembering therefore, holy and righteous Father, the sufferings and death of Thy Son, we proclaim that Christ is our true sacrifice, pure and spotless, offered once for all. We celebrate also His victorious resurrection and His ascension in glory. And we await His return with joy. It is in the name of this sovereign High Priest who now appears before Thy throne for us, that we present ourselves before Thee. Accept in His name our sacrifice of praise, and may our service be the living offering which Thou dost demand."

[1] The biblical understanding of prayer requires notice here. Prayer is first of all praise of God for His wondrous works, and this act of praise, presented as a memorial, becomes a plea that the Lord will deign to renew His blessings. The eucharistic prayer, beginning with the note of praise in the preface, follows the same pattern. It should also be noted that biblical prayer is rather an anamnesis of the Lord's wonderful works than a thanksgiving for His blessings (*Revue Biblique*, LXV, 1958, pp. 397 f.). Thus when Abraham's servant, in the presence of Rebekah,

THE WORDS OF CHRIST AT THE LAST SUPPER

is a complete historical sequence of events, relating to the creation and to redemption, running throughout the anaphora or eucharistic prayer. Thus in the liturgy of St. James, of Syrian provenance, the preface makes remembrance of the creation, both visible and invisible, and this leads up to the Sanctus. The Postsanctus declares the creation of man, the law, the incarnation, the life of Christ, and leads up to the institution narrative. There follows the anamnesis of the passion, cross and death, of the burial, resurrection, ascension, session, return and judgment. Next there is the Epiclesis which is a kind of solemn memorial of the role of the Holy Spirit in the Eucharist, as throughout the whole economy of redemption—the law, the prophets, the New Testament, the baptism of Christ and Pentecost. In this way the memorial is presented as a vast canvas depicting the creation and redemption, throughout the whole eucharistic prayer, apart from the interruption for the Sanctus, sung by all creatures visible and invisible, and the institution narrative. The same sequence, although even more developed, can be seen in the anaphora of St. Basil, of which the preface is a great thanksgiving to the Trinity adored by all the angelic powers. Although it has an analogous pattern, the anaphora of St. Chrysostom is much shorter, but the eucharistic prayer of all these Eastern anaphoras is closely unified by the historical sequence of the memorial. These fixed prayers present the whole mystery of creation and redemption at every celebration.

In the West, where there is a preference for short and compact prayers, the anamnesis contains the principal mysteries of Christ, but the variable preface provides an occasion for others. Thus, although the unity of the mysteries in the memorial is less in evidence than in the East, each separate mystery is given a eucharistic setting according to the liturgical year and the "colour" of the memorial is given greater emphasis on each feast day.[1] The correspondence between the gospel

recognizes that God has heard his prayer, his thanksgiving consists of an act of adoration of God and of praise for His wonderful works: "And the man bowed his head, and worshipped the Lord. And he said, Blessed be the Lord, the God of my master Abraham, who hath not forsaken his mercy and his truth towards my master" (Gen. 24: 26 f.).

[1] The word "colour" is not just figurative. In the Western rite the changing of the colours, according to the mystery celebrated, corresponds to the conception of the memorial which is developed by stages throughout the liturgical year. In the East liturgical colours are used much less; this may correspond to the presence of the whole mystery in each celebration. It is true that the liturgical year is observed but each celebration is a kind of Easter.

for the day and the proper preface emphasizes the correspondence between the proclamation of the mystery by the Word and the memorial of the mystery in the Sacrament. The Ambrosian liturgy, which has a proper preface for every Sunday and feast day, calls especial attention to this correspondence. So on Advent VI, when the Ambrosian liturgy celebrates the Annunciation, there is a very beautiful preface which connects the subject of the Gospel with the Eucharist and presents the mystery revealed by the Word under the form of a thanksgiving: "From her womb a fruit has burst forth which has replenished us by giving itself as the Bread of heaven."[1]

Although they vary less frequently and are less rich in content, the Roman prefaces are not less beautiful, being closely connected with the Gospel. Their sobriety is perhaps more suitable to our disturbed spirits in a distracted century. Thus, on Ascension Day, in the preface which glorifies God and invokes the angelic powers in the usual manner, we have: "who after his most glorious resurrection manifestly appeared to all his apostles, and in their sight ascended up into heaven to make us partakers in his divinity." This thanksgiving for the ascension also includes a recalling of our life which is hidden in Christ with God. We praise God for the ascension and at the same time we ask Him to make our participation in the Son's divinity effective in our lives through the Eucharist. If the gospel proclaims to the Church the mystery of Christ, the preface, which is co-ordinated with it, presents to God the Church's thanksgiving for this mystery and recalls to Him the fruits of this mystery promised to men.

The preface, the anamnesis and indeed the whole eucharistic prayer is an act of praise towards God for His covenant with men, and a recalling to God of that covenant, as the Psalmist sang:

> Yet God is my King of old,
> Working salvation in the midst of the earth.
> Thou didst divide the sea by thy strength . . .
> Thou . . . thou . . .
> Remember this . . . have respect unto the covenant . . .
> Arise, O God, plead thine own cause . . .
> Remember . . . Forget not . . . (Ps. 74: 12–23).

Like the Psalmist's prayer, the eucharistic prayer recalls the history of salvation, and in consideration of that history of the merciful acts

---

[1] "*De cuius ventre fructus effloruit, qui panis angelici munere nos replevit.*" *Messale ambrosiano*, Milan, 1954, p. 53.

of the Lord, it asks Him to recall and not to forget, to have respect unto the covenant, to arise and to plead. Admittedly the Church's memorial is one of grace while the Psalmist recalls the wicked that he may be avenged upon them, but the spiritual impulse is the same: "In consideration of what Thou hast done in history, because of the covenant, remember Thy people and Thy love for it; arise, O Lord, and plead as our Protector."[1]

Other solemn thanksgivings, which have the form of a eucharistic preface, express the same memorial of the wonderful works of God. One of the most beautiful is that for the paschal Vigil, the *Exultet*.[2] The blessing of the baptismal water in the Roman rite is also very rich from the point of view of the memorial.[3] The memorial of creation, the wilderness, Cana, the walking on the water, the baptism in the Jordan, the side of Christ pierced by the soldier's spear and the command to the disciples to baptize—all these are mysteries of salvation-history, upon which the Church's prayer is based to ask the Lord: "May the power of the Holy Spirit descend into this water . . . may the stain of all sins be here blotted out."[4] Whenever the Church gives thanks, it is simply asking God to bless His people again, according to His Word and covenant, in the mystery of His eternal and changeless love. It was in this way that the Psalmist prayed:

> Remember, O Lord, thy tender mercies and thy loving kindnesses;
> For they have been ever of old (Ps. 25: 6).

And the prophet Habakkuk cries out:

> O Lord, I have heard the report of thee, and am afraid:
> O Lord, revive thy work in the midst of the years,
> In the midst of the years make it known;
> In wrath remember mercy (3: 2).

---

[1] The liturgy of the first-fruits, recorded in Deuteronomy (26: 1–11), may be regarded as a kind of memorial of thanksgiving which foreshadows the eucharistic prayer. The believer brings the first-fruits to the priest and says: "I profess this day unto the Lord thy God, that I am come unto the land which the Lord sware unto our fathers for to give us." The priest takes the offering and places it in front of the altar while the believer utters a kind of anamnesis: "A wandering Aramean was my father . . ." He recalls the suffering in Egypt and the deliverance. Then he worships before Yahweh his God.

[2] *Verbum Caro*, 42, 1957, pp. 142 ff.

[3] *Ibid.*, 44, 1957, pp. 361 f.

[4] *"Descendat in hanc plenitudinem fontis virtus Spiritus Sancti . . . Hic omnium peccatorum maculae deleantur."*

This is exactly the meaning of the memorial—to ask God to revive His work and make it known that He may remember to have mercy.

The same memorial celebrated by Christ when He instituted the Eucharist continues to be celebrated by the Church. It uses the same elements; it performs the same actions; it utters the same words as it celebrates the same memorial of thanksgiving and intercession of the Son before the Father in the unity of the Spirit. It becomes one, in the mystery, with the events of the passion, resurrection and ascension, as Christ Himself, in the mystery, became one with the passion He was about to suffer, and with the resurrection and ascension which were soon to consummate His passion. Hence at the Eucharist the Church is in the same situation as Christ, in relation to His passion, resurrection and ascension. From the temporal point of view, the Church acts after these events as He acted before them. But, from the point of view of the mystery, which telescopes and unites the salvation events divided though they be by time, the Church actually lives the passion, resurrection and ascension; it presents the memorial of redemption and enjoys its fruits in the Eucharist now, as Christ lived the passion, resurrection and ascension and virtually offered beforehand, at the Last Supper, that life which He had undertaken to sacrifice to the Father on man's behalf. It is of course true that the sacrifice of the cross did not begin at the Last Supper, any more than it is extended in the Church's Eucharist—the sacrifice of the cross is unique. But He is present and is presented in memorial at the Eucharist, as He was present and was sacramentally offered at the Last Supper. Christ then undertook, by means of the sacramental signs, to give His body and to shed His blood, and the disciples received the fruits of this sacrifice, even before it was accomplished, because its entire reality was present and offered in the very person of Jesus as He accepted the redemptive death. Hence, at the Last Supper Christ presented to the Father the memorial of that sacrifice to which He had already consented, and at the Eucharist today the Church presents to the Father the memorial of that bloody sacrifice and of the heavenly intercession of the Son, and it distributes the fruits to the faithful. Both Christ's celebration in the upper room and those of the Church draw their meaning and efficacy from the unique and perfect sacrifice of the cross.[1]

[1] The Council of Trent clearly emphasizes the difference as well as the indissoluble unity between the Last Supper and Christ's death on the cross. "*Etsi semel seipsum in ara crucis, morte intercedente, Deo Patri, oblaturus erat ut . . . , corpus et sanguinem suum sub speciebus panis et vini Deo Patri obtulit ac sub earumdem rerum*

THE BLESSING OF THE ELEMENTS

Both in taking the bread and in taking the cup Jesus uttered a thanksgiving (εὐλογήσας, εὐχαριστήσας).[1] Quite obviously in order to appreciate the full meaning of this blessing or thanksgiving over the bread and the cup consideration must be given to the liturgical blessings over the bread and the cup of blessing at the Passover. The blessing over the bread was quite short: the father blessed God "who bringest forth bread from the earth".[2] Perhaps a special act of praise was added for the Passover. The blessing over the cup was more developed and explicit—this was a blessing that brought the meal to an end.

> *The father:* Bless ye our God to whom belongeth that which we
> have eaten.
> *Those present:* Blessed be our God for the food which we have
> eaten.

The father then takes the cup of blessing, raises it and, with his eyes fixed upon it, says the following blessing in the name of all:

> Blessed be thou, Yahweh our God, King of the world, who feedest
> the entire world with goodness, grace and loving-kindness.
> We thank thee, Yahweh our God, because thou hast given us as a
> heritage a good and ample land.
> Have mercy, Yahweh our God, upon Israel thy people,
> upon Jerusalem thy city,
> upon Zion the abiding place of thy glory,
> and upon thine altar and thy Temple.
> Blessed be thou, Yahweh, who dost build Jerusalem.[3]

We must note that while he said the blessing, he elevated the cup and looked at it. The thanksgiving accompanies a symbolic action;

---

symbolis apostolis . . . tradidit . . ."—"Although He had to offer Himself once to God the Father, while interceding by His death, on the altar of the cross, in order that . . . , He offered His body and blood to God the Father under the species of bread and wine, and under these same symbols distributed them to the apostles." *Sessio* XXII. C. 1.

[1] On the Semitic character of εὐλογήσας and the more Greek form of εὐχαριστήσας see Jeremias, *op. cit.,* p. 119. For the words of institution as a whole see *ibid.,* pp. 106–27.

[2] *Berakoth,* 6: 1.

[3] The text probably used at the time of Jesus has been analysed and formulated by L. Finkelstein, "The Birket ha-mazon", *Jewish Quarterly Review,* 1928–29, pp. 211–62.

there is a relation between the prayer and the cup; thanksgiving is rendered to God because it is the cup of salvation:

> I will take the cup of salvation,
> And call upon the name of the Lord (Ps. 116: 13).

The verb to bless, *berak*, is often used without an object in Hebrew, and this Semitism is noticeable in the absolute use of εὐλογεῖν (*eulogein*) in the blessing of the bread (Mk. 14: 22; Matt. 26: 26), where it is found without an object, contrary to normal Greek usage: "Jesus took bread, and when he had blessed, he brake it." A similar blessing without a specified object is used for the cup with the form *eucharistesas* (Mk. 14: 23; Matt. 26: 27; used in connexion with the bread by Luke and Paul, Lk. 22: 19; 1 Cor. 11: 24): "And he took a cup, and when he had given thanks, he gave to them." Thus the thanksgiving or blessing of the cup, like that of the bread, did not consist in "a consecration of matter in a magical sense", but in an act of praise to God for the cup of salvation, and similarly for the bread. My intentions should not be misinterpreted; they are neither polemical nor aimed at the Catholic doctrine and liturgy. I only wish to make clear that according to the thought and practice of the Jews, which provide the background to the Last Supper, Christ did not perform "a consecration of matter in a magical sense", but blessed or gave thanks for the bread and the cup, with the bread and the cup, and that by His actions He brought the bread and the cup into the blessing or thanksgiving as signs. To designate this specific and unique action, a technical term must be used which avoids the ideas of "magic" and "occasionalism"— these words will be considered later. It may be said that Christ "eucharistized" the bread and the wine, the term being used in order to exclude both magic and pure symbolism. This statement does not of course affect the doctrine of the real presence which will be examined below. It is made in order to define the meaning of the eucharistic prayer, which involves the bread and the wine in the memorial by "eucharistizing" them. This statement also helps us to see that the consecration should not be limited to a single point of time, since the whole eucharistic prayer, from the preface to the conclusion, "eucharistizes" the bread and the wine for the purposes of communion.

Not only is "magic" to be avoided, but also "occasionalism" or sacramental "symbolism". Christ did not utter a thanksgiving on the occasion of a brotherly meal at which moving symbols were present. Like the father of a Jewish family, He took the bread, elevated the cup, fixed His eyes upon it and pronounced the blessing—the Eucharist. The bread and the wine are an integral part of the thanksgiving; they are themselves the Eucharist which the words make explicit. There is an indissoluble connexion between Christ's words and the elements. Without the use of any magic, the words of Christ, i.e. His thanksgiving, had their effect upon the bread and the wine; they eucharistized them and were joined to them in order to constitute the Eucharist as a memorial of thanksgiving and intercession. That is why St. Paul could use the technical term, to bless, *berak*, *eulogein*, with the cup as a direct object: "The cup of blessing which we bless, is it not a communion of the blood of Christ?" (1 Cor. 10: 16). This is not just a question of altering a curious Semitism nor of adding an object to the Greek verb which the Hebrew does not have.[1] In the account of the feeding of the multitude the verb to bless, *eulogein*, has a direct object: "and having blessed them (the fish), he commanded . . ." (Mk. 8: 7). St. Luke writes: "And he took the five loaves and the two fishes, and looking up to heaven, he blessed them,[2] and brake; and gave to the disciples to set before the multitude" (9: 16). Two other passages are somewhat ambiguous in their use of *eulogein*. Mk. 6: 41 should probably be understood to mean "he blessed and broke the loaves", and Matt. 14: 19 "he pronounced the blessing, and having broken them, he gave the loaves to the disciples".

There is indeed a certain difficulty in the translation and use of an Hebraic form of blessing for food.[3] Yet there are examples of the blessing of things when the verb to bless, *berak* (LXX *eulogein*) is followed by a direct object, e.g. "God blessed (*iebarek*, *eulogesen*) the seventh day, and hallowed it" (Gen. 2: 3)—in this instance the blessing of the Sabbath corresponds to a kind of "depositing" of the Lord's holiness on the day of rest. There is a similar use in connexion with "a field which the Lord hath blessed" (Gen. 27: 27). Again God promises His people that He will bless their bread and water upon their settlement in Canaan: "and ye shall serve the Lord your God, and he shall bless thy bread, and thy water, and I will take sickness away from the

---

[1] Jeremias, *op. cit.*, p. 119, referring to Mk. 8: 7; Lk. 9: 16, goes too far in his linguistic considerations and forgets both the Hebrew and Greek background to the Septuagint.

[2] Some manuscripts read "on them" and this affirms the Semitic character of the blessing: "he pronounced the blessing on them" (*D. it. sy.*).

[3] εὐλογεῖν also designates the blessing of persons (Lk. 2: 34; 6: 28; 24: 50; Acts 3: 26; Rom. 12: 14; Eph. 1: 3; Heb. 6: 14; 7: 1, 6; 11: 20; 1 Peter 3: 9) like *berak* in the Old Testament (Gen. 27: 4; 48: 9; Prov. 30: 11, etc.).

midst of thee" (Ex. 23 : 25). Thus the blessing of food will take away all harmful elements, conferring purity upon them and thus avoiding all danger of evil. In Deut. 28: 12 God blesses all the work of men's hands by giving rain. In 1 Sam. 9: 13 there is a reference to the blessing of a sacrifice which is the object of the Hebrew verb: "for the people will not eat until he come, because he doth bless the sacrifice (*iebarek ha-zebach;* LXX, *eulogei ten thusian*); and afterwards they eat that be bidden." In all these cases the Septuagint translates *berak* with a direct object by *eulogein* with an accusative. So the New Testament writers were making no innovation in using *eulogein* with a direct object for the Jewish blessing over food; they were only interpreting this blessing in the light of the Old Testament passages just quoted. The blessing *for* food is also the blessing *over* food and the blessing *of* food.

The blessing for the bread and the cup both at the Passover and the Last Supper is then a thanksgiving to God united to and expressed by the elements, in such a way that by blessing God the elements are also blessed and that by thanking God the elements are "eucharistized". The passage of St. Paul already mentioned should therefore be understood as follows: "The cup of blessing, over which we proclaim thanksgiving to God and which we eucharistize, is it not a communion of the blood of Christ?" (1 Cor. 10: 16.)[1]

From the consideration of the meaning of the act of blessing or thanksgiving, we now turn to its verbal content in the Passover ritual in order to make explicit the meaning of Christ's Eucharist, and therefore that of the Church. The text of the thanksgiving over the cup, quoted above, consists of three sections. First, there is a blessing of Yahweh: "King of the world, who feedest the entire world with goodness, grace and loving-kindness." Then, the second section contains a thanksgiving to Yahweh "because thou hast given us as a heritage a good and ample land". Finally, the third section is a supplication on Israel's behalf, as well as for Jerusalem, Zion, the altar and the Temple, an intercession for the people, the city and Yahweh's

---

[1] Calvin (*Sermon 7 on I Corinthians*, 1558) has this comment on the saying: "There is a special blessing in the Supper in that the bread and the wine presented unto us are as it were pledges of the body and blood of our Lord Jesus Christ . . . Therefore the cup must be sanctified in accordance with this practice and similarly the bread: it is in order that the wine may be a figure of the blood of our Lord Jesus Christ and the bread of His body . . . We see therefore that St. Paul was not referring to a common blessing, such as may be used daily when we eat and drink, but he was speaking of what we must do when we have recourse to the sacraments."

dwelling place. And the prayer concludes with a further blessing of Yahweh "who dost build Jerusalem". The intercession is therefore part of the thanksgiving for the cup at the paschal meal and the supplication follows the blessing. As he lifts the cup of salvation and fixes his gaze upon it, the father blesses God for the food, thanks God for the land and intercedes with God for the people. This is what Jesus did also with the cup of blessing at the Last Supper: "Blessed be thou, Yahweh our God ... We thank thee, Yahweh our God ... Have mercy, Yahweh our God." Like Jesus, the Church at the Eucharist lifts the cup of salvation and blesses God by thanking Him and pleading with Him for His people, the Body of Christ. Thus the blessing for the paschal cup included both thanksgiving and intercession and, within the Passover context where it ought to be placed, the blessing for the eucharistic cup involves not only thanksgiving but also intercession for the Body of Christ which is the New Israel, the people of God, the new Jerusalem, the city of God, the new Zion, the dwelling place of the divine glory, the new Temple of the Lord—it is a prayer for the Church and a prayer for its future within the Kingdom of God.

THE BREAKING OF THE BREAD

In St. Matthew's account of the Last Supper great stress is laid on the action of breaking the bread: "Jesus took bread, and blessed, and brake it; and he gave it to the disciples, and said, Take, eat; this is my body" (26: 26).[1] St. Paul likewise emphasizes the fraction: "The bread which we break, is it not a communion of the body of Christ?" (1 Cor. 10: 16). In view of this insistence upon the fraction, which was a practical action for the purposes of distribution, it must be deemed to have a meaning in relation to the sacrifice of Christ. St. Luke writes: "This is my body which is given for you." St. Paul has only "for you". However, this short form in St. Paul is impossible in Aramaic and very difficult in Greek, which is why certain manuscripts have added "broken, given" as in St. Luke. The saying over the bread thus establishes very clearly a connexion between the fraction and the

[1] The whole emphasis is laid upon "he broke it", ἔκλασεν, by the connexion between the participles λαβών . . . καὶ εὐλογήσας, and by the use of yet another participle, δούς instead of ἔδωκεν (Mark and Luke). There is no doubt that the fraction is primarily a utilitarian action, since it is necessary to divide the bread amongst all present. The fraction has therefore primarily a community meaning, emphasized elsewhere by St. Paul (1 Cor. 10: 17). But, according to the words of Christ, this functional rite has assumed a sacrificial significance, which is the only one we have to consider here.

47

sacrifice of the cross: "This is my body broken (given) for you." This is the reading adopted by Calvin and he has a remarkable comment upon it:

"For myself, while acknowledging that Paul has made allusion to the breaking of the bread, yet I take broken to be used here in the sense of sacrificed; certainly this is not the proper use of the word, but it is not out of place. For even if 'not a bone of him' was damaged, yet, since His body was exposed first of all to so much torture and suffering, and then to the punishment of death in its cruellest form, it cannot be said that it was uninjured. That is what Paul means by its being broken. This, however, is the second part of the promise, and it must be not passed over lightly. For the Lord does not offer His body to us, just His body with nothing else said about it, but His body as having been sacrificed for us. The first part, then, tells us that His body is held out to us; this second part brings out what we come to enjoy through it, viz. a share in redemption, and the application to us of the benefit of His sacrifice. That is why the Supper is a mirror which represents Christ crucified to us, so that a man cannot receive the Supper and enjoy its benefits, unless he embraces Christ crucified."[1]

Many Reformed Liturgies preserve this longer reading in Paul as a formula accompanying the fraction: "The bread which we break is a communion of the body of our Lord Jesus Christ who was broken for us."[2]

The fraction of the bread may then be taken to signify the Body of Christ *given* or *broken*. The fraction is indeed an action which represents and presents the sacrifice of the Lord, i.e. the gift of Himself to men at the Last Supper, as at each Eucharist, because of the unique gift of the cross. The first three Evangelists designate the wine as the blood of Christ and the foundation of the new covenant "shed for many" (Lk. "for you"). The presence of the sacrifice under the sacramental sign is again evident. The participle is used with an immediate future sense, so that "given" and "shed" are to be understood as "which is about to be given . . . which is about to be shed." The bread and the wine are thus placed in a sacramental relationship to the sacrifice of the cross. The Last Supper, celebrated by Christ, is truly the sacrament of His sacrifice, the previously given sign of the present efficacy of His unique oblation. Similarly the Church's Eucharist is truly the sacrament of the

[1] *The First Epistle of Paul the Apostle to the Corinthians*, trans. J. W. Fraser, 1960, p. 248.
[2] *Liturgie de l'Eglise Réformée de France*, 1955, p. 41.

sacrifice of Christ, the perpetually given sign of the present efficacy of the unique oblation of Christ to His Father.

The bread and the wine are said by Christ to be His body and blood. He does not say that the action of breaking the bread is His body given nor that the pouring of the wine into the cup is His blood shed. The saying "This is my body given" was uttered at the distribution and not at the fraction since it begins with the word "take" (Matt. "Take, eat"). Similarly the saying "This is my blood shed" was uttered at the distribution ("Drink ye all of this"), and this was separated from the action of pouring the wine into the cup of blessing by the words of the blessings, as was customary at the Passover. "This" therefore refers to the element of bread and to the element of wine and not to the actions of breaking and pouring. It is the bread which is the body of Christ and the wine which is His blood. But by declaring the bread to be His body and the wine His blood, Christ recalls the actions which have just been performed: the bread has been broken and the wine poured out. Hence the bread and wine are not the body and blood of Christ from the point of view of their material nature but in accordance with the action of sacrifice itself. The bread is the body of Christ *given* in sacrifice and the wine is His blood *shed* in sacrifice.

The Lord's words "This is my body . . . This is my blood" refer to the bread and the wine not only as elements but also as signifying the sacrifice of Christ by means of a symbolic action. When the Lord says: "This is my body given", there is a reference both to the bread as the body and to the action which signifies Christ's self-giving in sacrifice, i.e. to the fraction. Similarly, in the words for the cup, there is a reference both to the wine as the blood and to the action which signifies Christ's self-giving in sacrifice, i.e. to the pouring of the wine into the cup before the thanksgiving. At the Eucharist at the present day, these symbolic actions take place before the repetition of the Lord's words. The fraction precedes the communion and therefore has a primary reference to the community—the body of Christ is divided amongst all the members. It is to be desired that the fraction should have a closer connexion with Christ's words and it would seem right for the celebrant, as he reads the institution narrative, to perform the actions of Christ and so to have a first fraction which would make the sacrificial meaning clear. The second fraction, before communion, would then have the community reference already mentioned.

The symbolism of the shedding of the blood is more difficult to express, since Christ's words over the wine did not immediately follow the action of pouring the wine into the cup. This action, prior to the thanksgiving at the Passover, is the basis of what takes place at the offertory. Before the eucharistic prayer, the elements are brought to the altar and the wine is poured into the cup. This action, according to Christ's own words, is symbolic of sacrifice and it therefore unites the offertory, which is a symbol of the Church's sacrifice, with the eucharistic prayer, which is the memorial of Christ's sacrifice. The pouring of the wine into the cup at the offertory provides a link between the offering of the Church and the memorial of the Lord, which the offering indeed becomes, in the eucharistic prayer. In the Ambrosian rite this symbolic connexion between the pouring of the wine into the cup and the sacrifice of the cross is brought out in the repetition by the priest, as he pours out wine and then water, of John 19: 34: "From the side of Christ there came out blood, and water likewise, in the name of the Father and of the Son and of the Holy Spirit." In the rite of Lyons there is added to this reference to the sacrifice of the cross (Jn. 19: 34) a further reference to the mystery of the Trinity, based upon 1 Jn. 5: 6–8 and the Vulgate gloss:[1] "From the side of our Lord Jesus Christ there came out blood and water for the redemption of the world at the hour of the passion; it is the mystery of the Holy Trinity; John the Evangelist beheld it and bore witness to it, and we know that his witness is true."

In the Roman rite this action is accompanied by a prayer which directs attention to the participation of our human nature in the "divine nature of Him who vouchsafed to become partaker of our human nature, Jesus Christ". The mingling of water and wine was a Greek custom practised in Palestine in the first century A.D.,[2] and from an early date this was interpreted as a symbol of the union of our human nature with the Godhead of Christ.[3] Here again we have an expression of the idea that the Church's sacrifice, i.e. the offertory, is

---

[1] "This is he that came by water and blood . . . And it is the Spirit that beareth witness . . . For there are three that bear record (in heaven, the Father, the Word, and the Holy Ghost: and these three are one. And there are three that bear witness in earth), the Spirit, and the water, and the blood: and these three agree in one" (So A.V.).

[2] Strack-Billerbeck, IV, pp. 613 ff. Reference is made to this mixture by Justin, *Apol.*, I, 65; 67.

[3] "The Ebionites, who do not receive by faith into their soul the union of God and man . . . reject the commixture of the heavenly wine, and wish it to be the water of the world only, not receiving God so as to have union with Him" (Irenaeus, *Adv. Haer.*, V. 1, 3).

linked with the memorial of Christ's sacrifice in the eucharistic prayer. The mixture of the water and the wine symbolizes the humanity of the Church and its offering taken up by the Godhead of Christ and His sacrifice; hence Cyprian states: "If anyone offers wine only, the blood of Christ is dissociated from us; but if the water be alone, the people are dissociated from Christ."[1] The preparation of the chalice thus establishes a link between the offertory and the memorial of the sacrifice. The pouring of the wine into the cup (as in the Passover ritual) provides the symbolism of Christ's words: "This is my blood shed . . ."; the mixture of water and wine (as in several rites) constitutes the symbol of the union of humanity with God and (in the Roman rite) of the Church's offering with Christ's sacrifice or (as in the Ambrosian rite and the rite of Lyons) the symbol of Christ's pierced side, thus making the offertory an anticipation of the cross.[2]

The words of Christ, which make the bread and the wine His body and blood, refer to the one as given and to the other as shed, thus anticipating the sacrifice of the cross, and this is symbolized by the fraction and by pouring the wine into the cup. The bread and wine are thus truly the sacrament of the body and blood of the Crucified One and so the sacrament of His presence and sacrifice.[3]

THE SEPARATION OF THE ELEMENTS

The separation of the body and blood of Christ under the two elements of bread and wine is another symbol of the presence of the sacrifice at the Eucharist that must not be overlooked. The Aramaic expression *bisra udema*, flesh-blood, in Greek $\sigma\tilde{\omega}\mu\alpha$-$\alpha\tilde{\iota}\mu\alpha$, refers to the two elements that make up the body, especially the body of a victim,

[1] *Ep.* 63: 13. Luther rejected the mingling of water and wine as to him it signified an impossible union of humanity and the purity of God (*Formula missae et communionis*, 16). Hence the Council of Trent considered it necessary to uphold this practice (*Sessio XXII. C. 7*).

[2] In the East the mixture of water and wine signifies not only the water and blood from the side of Christ but also the union of the two natures in Christ; hence the Armenian monophysites do not observe the custom. The practice was upheld by Trent for three reasons: i. Christ Himself did it. ii. It recalls the water and blood from the side of Christ. iii. Since the waters in Revelation (17: 15) represent the peoples, the mingling may be taken to represent the union of the faithful with their Head (*Sessio XXII. C. 7*).

[3] The use of *red* wine at the Last Supper would also remind the disciples of sacrificial blood, and indeed a comparison between red wine and blood is frequent in the Old Testament, e.g. "He hath washed his garments in wine, and his vesture in the blood of grapes" (Gen. 49: 11; cf. Deut. 32: 14).

which are separated in the act of sacrifice: "But flesh (*basar*) with the life (*nephesh*, soul) thereof, which is the blood (*dam*) thereof, shall ye not eat . . . For the life of the flesh is in the blood" (Gen. 9: 4; Lev. 17: 11; cf. Deut. 12: 23; Ez. 39: 17 f.).[1] In the New Testament there is one passage where the double expression σῶμα-αἷμα, body-blood, is used of the two constituent elements of a sacrificial victim: "For the *bodies* (σώματα) of those beasts, whose *blood* is brought into the holy place by the high priest as an offering for sin, are burned without the camp" (Heb. 13: 11).[2] It is therefore evident that Christ's use of bread and wine as signs of His body and blood at the Last Supper would suggest a sacrifice to the disciples. With their Hebraic mode of thought they could scarcely think otherwise. When Christ said: "*den bisri*, this is my body . . . *den idemi*, this is my blood", the disciples had before them the signs of a sacrifice. As they partook of the Passover, they would see in the bread and the wine, which were the body and blood of Christ, the ancient sacrificial Lamb and the new paschal Lamb which was to be sacrificed, i.e. Christ Himself. They communicated in the sacrifice of the cross which was sacramentally present and they received its fruits by anticipation.

In the Synoptic tradition the connexion between the Last Supper and the meal at which the paschal Lamb was eaten is emphasized; in the Johannine tradition the connexion between the death of Christ and the sacrifice of the paschal Lamb is emphasized.[3] In the Eucharist the Church recognizes the extension of these two traditions in the sacrament of the sacrifice of the paschal Lamb, i.e. Christ sacrificed upon the cross. The signs of the presence of Christ sacrificed are recognized in the Lord's body and blood separated like the body and blood of a sacrificial victim, like the body and blood of the paschal Lamb. Thus in the very existence of these two elements, the eucharistized bread and wine, we have the sacrament of the sacrifice of the cross, because we have the sacrament of the separated body and blood of Christ, i.e.

[1] In these passages *basar* is translated in the LXX by σάρξ, flesh, or κρέας, meat. *Basar* is translated 143 times by σάρξ and 23 times by σῶμα. Σῶμα is always used for *basar*, except where it means a "corpse". Hence there is no difficulty in the assumption that σῶμα is a translation of the Aramaic *bisra* and that this was the term employed by Jesus.

[2] Heb. 13: 11 refers to Lev. 16: 27 and translates *basar* (LXX κρέας) by σῶμα.

[3] A. Jaubert, *La date de la Cène*, 1957; "Le calendrier des Jubilés et de la secte de Qumran. Ses origines bibliques", *V.T.*, III, 1953, pp. 250–64; "La date de la dernière Cène", *R.H.R.*, CXLVI, 1954, pp. 140–73; "Le calendrier des Jubilés et les jours liturgiques de la semaine", *V.T.*, VII, 1957, pp. 35–61.

the sacrament of a victim that has been sacrificed. When it breaks the bread and utters the words of Christ: "This is my body given", and when it raises the cup containing the poured-out wine and utters the words of Christ: "This is my blood shed", the Church makes the sacrifice of the cross present, in all its redemptive, sanctifying and saving power, under the separated signs of the bread and the wine, which are the body and blood of Christ, separated at the time of the sacrifice on the cross.

The question is sometimes asked why Christ has instituted the sacrament of the Eucharist under two elements. Communion is obediently administered in both kinds, but it is difficult to see what is added by the cup. If the Eucharist were only the sacrament of Christ's real presence, it would be quite sufficient to communicate in one kind only. Christ cannot be divided, and Catholic theologians are right in affirming that Christ is wholly present in either element. But the Eucharist, while it is the sacrament of the real presence, is also the sacrament of Christ's sacrifice, being the sacrament of Christ's real presence in His sacrifice of the cross. The use of two elements is intelligible in the light of this fact. We make the memorial of the sacrifice of the cross and that is signified by the separation of the body and blood of Christ, and we communicate in that sacrifice by taking the bread and the wine, Christ's body and blood, separately. Our communion in both kinds is then a communion with Christ really present with His sacrifice and with all the power which flows from it, under the separated signs of the body and blood of the sacrificed paschal Lamb.[1]

The Blood of the Covenant

A further indication of the sacrificial character of the Eucharist is the reference to the blood of the covenant: "This is my blood of the

---

[1] Z. Ursinus, one of the authors of the *Catéchisme de Heidelberg*, in his Commentary on the twenty-eighth Sunday, qu. 75, par. II, says: "The wine is separated from the bread to signify the violence of Christ's death, when His blood was poured out and separated from His body." Communion in both kinds makes clearer our participation in Christ's sacrifice and prevents the division, still observable in Catholic circles, between presence at a sacrifice and communion in a sacrament. T. Maertens, "L'Histoire de la communion au service de sa pastorale", *Paroisse et Liturgie*, 1958, 5, p. 357, frankly acknowledges this fact. "Indeed, there is no sacrifice but that which is sacramental and there is no sacrament except by reference to the sacrifice of Christ. Although this truth remains fundamental, it was better symbolized when the faithful communicated in both kinds."

covenant, which is shed for many (Matt. 26: 28; Mk. 14: 24). This cup is the new covenant in my blood (Lk. 22: 20; I Cor. 11: 25), even that which is poured out for you" (Lk.). These two equivalent forms set forth the blood of Christ crucified as the blood that is to be shed to establish the new covenant of God with the many who are to be His people. On Sinai Yahweh's covenant with His people was sealed with the blood of victims. After he had received the law, Moses built an altar and ordered the people to offer burnt offerings and peace offerings. He collected the blood of the victims and sprinkled half of it upon the altar; then, after the reading of the book of the covenant, the people declared: "All that the Lord hath spoken will we do, and be obedient" (Ex. 24: 4–7). Moses then took the remaining half of the blood and sprinkled it on the people, saying: "Behold the blood of the covenant, which the Lord hath made with you concerning all these words" (24: 8). There can be no doubt that the reference to the blood of the new covenant at the Last Supper was an allusion to the old covenant, sealed with the blood of the sacrifices.

The rite of the covenant consisted in taking half of the blood and sprinkling the altar with it in order to give it to God as a sign of the covenant; then the other half was taken and sprinkled on the people in order to give it to them as a pledge of the covenant. Thus, by the blood of the sacrifice, the union of God and the people was sealed in a covenant. But this covenant was not established by a sacramental sign, the sacrificial blood, alone; it was also established and made dependent upon obedience to the Word of God: "Behold the blood of the covenant, which the Lord hath made with you concerning all these words." Hence the covenant with Yahweh, in the Old Testament, is concluded upon the basis of the Word of God which the people undertake to carry out and is sealed by the sign of the blood offered to Yahweh on the altar and to the people by the sprinkling. This is a semi-liturgical formula: (i) A sacrifice in which Moses presents the blood of the covenant to God upon the altar (vv. 5 f.). (ii) A reading of the Word of God by Moses from the book of the covenant (v. 7a). (iii) An undertaking by the people to obey, in the form of a response (v. 7b). (iv) A giving of the blood of the covenant by Moses to the people with the words: "Behold the blood of the covenant."

Under the new covenant Word and Sacrament are also equally united. Communion with God implies obedience to His Word as well as the reception of the body and blood of Christ. Christian worship also unites Word and Sacrament as two parts of one whole: the ministry of the Word and the ministry of the Sacrament. It is also to be noted that in the covenant rite on Sinai Moses presented the blood of the sacrifice to God before giving it to the people, and this reveals the essential feature of the covenant, viz. communion in the same blood which has been presented both to God and to the people. When Christ said: "This is my blood of the covenant, which is shed for many", He was presenting the sign of the sacrifice of the cross, when He would shed His blood before the Father, as Moses sprinkled the blood of the victims on the altar, and when He would shed it for the "many" that constitute the people of God. The cross is both the altar of God which receives the blood of the covenant and the place from which the many receive the sprinkling of that blood shed for them.

At the Last Supper Christ presented in advance the blood of His sacrifice to the Father; He offered Himself as the victim ready for the sacrifice of the new covenant; and He communicated in advance the blood of that new covenant in His imminent sacrifice to the disciples who represented the whole people. At the Eucharist the Church presents to the Father, under the sign of the wine, this blood of the new covenant shed on the cross, which has become an effective act of intercession on its behalf and upon which it rests its prayer; and it communicates this same blood of Christ to the faithful, who thereby renew their covenant with God, as they listen to the Word of God that they may be obedient to it. This new covenant, established in the blood of Christ which was poured out on the cross, and renewed in the same blood, given at the Eucharist, is the eschatological covenant prophesied by Jeremiah: "Behold, the days come, saith the Lord, that I will make a new covenant with the house of Israel, and with the house of Judah . . . I will forgive their iniquity, and their sin will I remember no more" (31: 31, 34). This eschatological promise was widely remembered at the time of Christ. At the Last Supper, by means which recalled the covenant on Sinai, He proclaimed that the new covenant would be continually established by a sacrifice, the signs of which were given beforehand in the separated elements of bread and wine, the latter being His blood of the new covenant.

The foundation of this covenant was, according to Christ's words, to take place in the immediate future: the blood *is*, i.e. is about to be, shed. But the sign of the blood was already a communication by anticipation of the covenant, of its reality and of the fruits which it brings—pardon and the remission of sins. St. Paul reports Christ's words as having a present reference: "This cup *is* the new covenant in my blood" (1 Cor. 11: 25). This is another illustration of the way in which the sacrament can telescope moments separated in time and make present both future and past events. The Last Supper conveyed in advance the effects of the new covenant to the disciples: unity with God regained in the pardon and remission of sins. The Eucharist conveys the same effects of the new covenant to us at the present day: we are renewed in our union with God, who looks upon the blood of the covenant presented by us to Him and pardons our fault, remembering our offences no more.

THE REMISSION OF SINS

St. Matthew has transmitted an explicit statement on the subject of the divine forgiveness: "This is my blood of the new covenant, which is shed for many unto remission of sins." The Last Supper was the occasion of the reception by the disciples of the blood of the covenant; it was the sacrament of union with God, since the imminent sacrifice of the cross, the fruit of which they received in advance, was to be a sacrifice for the remission of sins: by His blood shed on the cross, Christ was going to reconcile man to God by blotting out the sin which divided them. The new covenant with God, reconciliation and union, these are the fruit of the remission of sins through the blood shed on the cross, the sacrament of which was distributed to the disciples at the Last Supper. The Eucharist, since it is the sacrament of the sacrifice of the cross, renews us in the covenant with God, in reconciliation and union with the Father, through the blood of Christ therein conveyed for the remission of sin. The cross alone *has established* the new covenant with God by the blood of Christ shed for the remission of sins, but the Eucharist at the present day *confirms* us in that covenant and re-establishes us in union with God by securing the remission of sins for us now. St. John has recorded Christ's words which emphasize the present reality of the remission of sins: "Whosesoever sins ye forgive, they are forgiven unto them; whosesoever sins ye retain, they are retained" (20: 23). This present remission derives from the cross and is conveyed to us by the Word and in the Sacraments: in baptism (Acts 2: 38), in the Eucharist (Matt. 26: 28), in absolution (Jn. 20: 23) and in the anointing of the sick (Jas. 5: 14 f.).

The words "unto remission of sins", recorded by St. Matthew, establish a connexion between the Last Supper and the sacrifice for sin on the great Day of Atonement (Lev. 16). In Hebrews there is a passage, which alludes to Leviticus 16: 27 and compares the sacrifice of Christ with the rite of atonement for sin—this has a bearing upon our understanding of the Eucharist. "We have an *altar*, whereof they have no right to *eat* which serve the tabernacle. For the *bodies* of those beasts, whose *blood* is *brought into the holy place* by the high priest *as an offering for sin*, are burned without the camp. Wherefore Jesus also, that he might sanctify the people through his own blood, suffered without the gate. Let us therefore go forth unto him without the camp, *bearing his reproach*. For we have not here an abiding city, but we seek after the city which is to come. Through him then *let us offer up a sacrifice of praise* to God *continually*, that is, the fruit of lips which make confession to his name. But to do good and to communicate forget not: for with such *sacrifices* God is well pleased" (13: 10–16). The use of liturgical terms in this passage establishes a connexion between sacrifice for sin, the sacrifice of the cross, the Eucharist and Christian life, which we must seek to understand.

The "altar" referred to is the cross of Christ on which His blood was shed. There is no suggestion of the eucharistic table—until the time of Cyprian, who uses the term for the table, "altar" had usually a symbolic sense and was applied to Christ, to the martyr or to the Christian. Our altar, the centre of worship, is the cross of Christ and Christ Himself, as Thomas Aquinas has so well expressed it: "This altar is either the cross of Christ, on which Christ was sacrificed for us, or Christ Himself in whom and by whom we offer our prayers." Those who serve the Tabernacle, in the Jewish cult, have no right to eat of this altar. The expression "to eat of the altar" is to be related to the expression "to have communion with the altar" (1 Cor. 10: 18) or "have a portion with the altar" (1 Cor. 9: 13). The right in question is the right to take part in the sacred meal which followed the sacrifice according to the Jewish ritual. Hence, the altar which we have and of which the Jews have not the right to eat is the cross of Christ, of which Christians have the right "to eat".

These expressions obviously involve an allusion to the Eucharist as the sacrament of the sacrifice of the cross and as the sacred meal of the new covenant. They indicate first a relationship between the altar and the sacred meal, i.e. between the cross and the Eucharist. Next there comes a reference to the sacrifice for sin on the Day of Atonement. The High Priest entered beyond the veil into the holy of holies, carrying the blood of the sin offering with which he performed the rite of atonement on the mercy-seat in a cloud of incense "because of the uncleannesses of the children of Israel, and because of their transgressions, even all their sins" (Lev. 16: 16). The rite of atonement for the people was performed in two stages: first the sacrifice for sin on the altar, then the sprinkling of the blood in the sanctuary, within the veil, on the mercy-seat. The author of Hebrews sees in this a symbol of two stages in Christ's work of expiation: the sacrifice for sin on the altar of the cross and the entrance into the heavenly sanctuary with the blood of the sacrifice as a continual act of intercession. Here we see the twofold aspect of the one and only sacrifice of Christ for the one and only remission of sins: an act in history and yet continual, once for all and yet never ending because once for all. The sacrificial character of the Eucharist for the remission of sins is to be connected with this entrance of Christ the High Priest into heaven, through the veil, bearing the blood of His sacrifice as a perpetual intercession. The blood of the Eucharist is this very blood that Christ bore from the cross into the heavenly sanctuary, and it is the symbol of His unceasing intercession for the remission of sins, for the present reconciliation and unity of all men with the Father. Within this context of the sin offering on the Day of Atonement, the body of Christ, sacrificed on the altar of the cross and presented in the Eucharist, would above all signify the unique historical offering of Christ for the remission of sins and the reconciliation with God of the whole people, and the blood of Christ, borne into the heavenly sanctuary and presented at the Eucharist, would signify the continual heavenly intercession of Christ that the remission of sins might be applied and unity with God might be renewed.

Just as the priests of the old covenant had no part in the sin offering for the people (Lev. 4: 21), so the Jews, if they remain within the narrow confines of ritual observance, have no part in the sacrifice of the cross and the Eucharist, which is the meal or sacrament of that sacrifice. The bodies of the victims, sacrificed as sin offerings, were burnt outside the camp. Jesus also suffered outside the gates of Jerusalem (Jn. 19: 17) to sanctify the people by His blood. He gave Himself entirely to God; He was completely "consumed" on the altar of the cross like a burnt offering, when the whole victim is burnt on the altar, "an offering made by fire, of a sweet savour unto the Lord" (Lev. 1: 9). This image presents yet another theme for consideration. To have a part in the sacrifice of the cross, it is necessary not only to leave the Jewish "camp" to join Christ at Golgotha, outside the city, on that cross which is the altar for the sin offering, but also it is necessary to leave the conditions of this world to join our High Priest in heaven whither He has borne His blood to sanctify the people of God. "Let us therefore go forth unto him without the camp, bearing his reproach" (v. 13), that is, go forth from Judaism which did not recognize Christ in order to fall down before the altar of the cross; and it is also to go forth out of the shackles of this world to join our heavenly High Priest in the midst of the saints, who worship the Lamb as it had been slain (Rev. 4: 6–10). "For we have not here an abiding city, but we seek after the city which is to come"—so Hebrews continues, giving a second eschatological sense to our "going forth from the camp". Christ has therefore not established a new form of earthly worship, a kind of competitor with the Jewish cultus, but after having accomplished the one and only sacrifice for sin He has carried the sign of it, His blood, into the heavenly holy of holies, the heavenly sanctuary, where, as High Priest, He intercedes for us amidst the saints and where all our worship and every Eucharist should join Him. His worship is then not another order of worship on the earth, it is the worship of heaven, unique and perfect, which truly glorifies the Lord: "For Christ entered not into a holy place made with hands, like in pattern to the true; but into heaven itself, now to appear before the face of God for us" (Heb. 9: 24).

The Eucharist should enable us to follow Christ the High Priest in His ascension, to pass with Him the doors of the heavenly sanctuary and, beyond the veil, to unite with His intercession, by the presentation of His sacrifice, in expectation of "the city which is to come". At the beginning of the eucharistic prayer, the celebrant invites the Church to "go forth without the camp of this world, without the gate", by the use of these words:

> Lift up your hearts.
> *We lift them up to the Lord.*
> Let us give thanks unto our Lord God.
> *It is meet and right so to do.*[1]

Christ, the High Priest, has gone up into heaven; He has crossed its threshold and passed the veil, and He now presents Himself with the blood, the sign of His sacrifice, before the face of God for us. Similarly, under the old covenant, the High Priest went up to the *Debir*, the seat of the Word of God, or holy of holies, and crossed its threshold and passed the veil (Ex. 26: 33; I Kings 6: 31; Lev. 16: 12–16), and presented

---

[1] The *Sursum corda* and its response the *Habemus ad Dominum* are the liturgical expression of the exhortation: "Let us therefore go forth unto him without the camp, bearing his reproach" (Heb. 13: 13).

himself with the blood of the sin offering before the face of God, veiled in a cloud of incense, to make atonement for the people. The liturgical image of the Old Testament has found its full reality in Christ. Entry into the holy of holies, which was forbidden the people of Israel, is now open to the Church through Christ: "Having therefore, brethren, boldness to enter into the holy place by the blood of Jesus, by the way which he dedicated for us, a new and living way, through the veil, that is to say, his flesh; and having a great high priest over the house of God; let us draw near with a true heart in fulness of faith, having our hearts sprinkled from an evil conscience, and our body washed with pure water" (Heb. 10: 19–22). By the flesh of Christ, sacrificed and living, by His humanity, which has passed through the veil of the heavenly sanctuary, and by the blood of Christ, shed for the establishment and consecration of the New Covenant and presented in intercession in the heavenly sanctuary, a free passage has been opened unto us towards God "unto the throne of grace, that we may receive mercy, and may find grace to help us in time of need" (Heb. 4: 16).[1]

In its worship and in its Eucharist, as in its life, the Church "goes forth" towards Christ "without the camp of this world", bearing the reproach of Christ. Although it is invited to join in the worship of heaven in anticipation of the city that is to come, it is not yet fully triumphant. At Golgotha and on the heavenly altar, the Church meets the sacrificed Lamb and it must bear His reproach, His cross: "Remember, Lord, the reproach of thy servants" (Ps. 89: 50).

As a consequence of this new heavenly worship, over which Christ presides and with which the Church associates its Eucharist, as it bears the cross of Christ, a new exhortation is made: "Through Him, let us carry as an offering to God a sacrifice of praise always, that is the fruit of lips confessing His Name." Because of the sacrifice and intercession of its High Priest, the Church is able to offer a sacrifice of praise, foretold in Lev. 7: 11, to thank God for His benefits, His acts of intervention, His mercy and His repeated acts of deliverance:

> Oh that men would praise the Lord for his goodness,
> And for his wonderful works to the children of men!
> And let them offer the sacrifices of thanksgiving,
> And declare his works with singing (Ps. 107: 21 f.).

The Church's Eucharist is also a sacrifice of praise; it is the fruit of lips

---

[1] For the difficult construction of Heb. 10: 19–22, see Spicq, *op. cit.*, pp. 315 f.

confessing the Name of the Lord, and it is accomplished in charity, in the sharing of goods, "for with such sacrifices God is well pleased". As it follows its High Priest in the heavenly worship, the Church, bearing its cross, offers its sacrifice of praise and its sacrifice of charity, which is one and the same sacrifice, to the glory of God: it offers its Eucharist and its service in one act of thanksgiving for all the blessings of God through His Christ.

The Eucharist, as a sacrifice of thanksgiving, presents the blood of Christ, which is the blood of the covenant, shed for many *unto remission of sins*. The connexion between this reference to the remission of sins and the Day of Atonement has already been noted. The Eucharist *presents* the blood of Christ, shed on the cross and borne into the heavenly sanctuary for the remission of sins. But the blood of Christ is alone effective; only His sacrifice on the cross, only His intercession in heaven, only the presence of His sacrifice and His intercession, can obtain the remission of sins for us. It has been seen that, according to Hebrews, the sin offering of the old covenant, and especially that of the Day of Atonement, was a memorial of sin, a solemn confession of sins before God without any certainty that they would be forgiven: "But in those sacrifices there is a remembrance made of sins year by year. For it is impossible that the blood of bulls and goats should take away sins" (Heb. 10: 3 f.). The High Priest made the anamnesis or memorial of sins by the sin offering; Christ remits sins by the sacrifice of the cross and the presentation of His blood in intercession in the heavenly sanctuary; the Church, in union with its heavenly High Priest, presents, at the Eucharist, the blood of Christ as a memorial or anamnesis of Him, of His sacrifice, and of His intercession, for the remission of sins.

It is to be noted that the same word is used for the memorial of sins by the Jewish High Priest (Heb. 10: 3) and for the memorial of Christ at the Eucharist (1 Cor. 11: 25). This emphasizes the comparison: on one side there is the memorial of sin, with no certainty of forgiveness, on the other the memorial of Christ, of His sacrifice and intercession, for the remission of sins; on one side the sin recalled to God by a solemn confession, on the other the sacrifice and intercession of Christ recalled to the Father by thanksgiving and intercession. Thus the blood presented at the Eucharist "as the memorial of Christ" (1 Cor. 11: 25) is also presented "unto remission of sins" (Matt. 26: 28). The two expressions "as the memorial" and "unto remission" are parallel; indeed the Church, at the Eucharist, presents to the Father the memorial of the Son, of His sacrifice and intercession and, as it gives thanks to Him, it intercedes for the remission of sins, for the reconciliation and union of men with God, by holding in its hands the cup of salvation, i.e. the cup of the new covenant which is the blood of Christ shed for many unto remission of sins. Christ Himself, when He instituted the Eucharist, raised the cup of salvation and uttered the blessing of the Passover ritual: "Have mercy, O Lord our God, upon Israel, thy people." And the Lord, who hearkened to the Son at the Last Supper and on the cross, hearkens to Him now in His heavenly intercession and, at the same time, hearkens to the Church which, in the Eucharist, presents the blood of Christ, the blood of the covenant shed for many unto remission of sins.

THE PRESENT REALITY OF THE SACRIFICE

The bread broken and given, the wine outpoured, the body and blood presented separately, the reference to the covenant in the blood and to the remission of sins are all signs of the sacrifice on the cross and of the intercession in heaven of the Church's High Priest. These recallings of the sin offering and the sprinkling in the holy of holies make the Eucharist the sacrament of the sin offering on the cross and of the intercession of the Son in the heavenly sanctuary. The Eucharist makes present the sacrifice for sin on the cross and the Son's intercession in heaven; the Church thereby enters into communion with the High Priest in His heavenly intercession, which makes both the sacrifice of the covenant and the sacrifice for sin, accomplished on the cross, present. With Him and in Him the Church presents this sacrifice to the Father, and so the broken bread and the poured out wine, signs of the sacrificed body and the blood that has been shed, intercede for the remission of sins and the needs of the whole people and, at the same time, give thanks for all the marvellous works that have been done.

This body given and this blood shed were given and shed in sacrifice on the cross "for many".[1] In the Eucharist this same body and this same blood, which are the sacrament of the presence of the sacrament of the cross, are presented to the Father in thanksgiving and intercession, in communion with the heavenly praise and intercession of the Son amidst the saints. "For you" or "for many" mean that even now the bread broken and given and the wine outpoured, which are the body and blood of the Son presented to the Father, are the effective inter-

[1] For the translation of $\pi\epsilon\rho\iota$ or $\upsilon\pi\grave{\epsilon}\rho\ \pi o\lambda\lambda\hat{\omega}\nu$, see Jeremias, *op. cit.*, pp. 123 ff.

cession of the Church for the faithful and for all mankind. The Church presents to the Father in intercession the signs or sacrament of the gift which the Son offered on the cross to the Father for us and for the many. And this sacrament of the gift offered by the Son to the Father is also the sacrament of the gift bestowed by God upon the faithful and upon all mankind. This gift is received by the Church in communion.

Consequently the memorial and the communion must not be separated; there must be no division between the sacrament of the Son offered to the Father and the sacrament of Christ's presence given to the Church. The Eucharist is an indivisible whole. The sacrament of the sacrifice to the Father and the sacrament of the presence in the Church is one and the same sacrament and must be so understood in the light of Jesus' prayer: "That they may all be one; even as thou, Father, art in me, and I in thee, that they also may be in us: that the world may believe that thou didst send me" (Jn. 17: 21). The gift of unity with the Father and the Son, which is the particular gift conveyed in the Eucharist, is connected with the unity of Father and Son in the incarnation and in the act of sacrifice; and the fruit of this unity is the evangelization of the world. The sacrament of the sacrifice and the sacrament of the presence are one in the Eucharist. Christ is present to His Church under the signs of His sacrifice to the Father, and the Church also presents the memorial of His sacrifice when it receives its crucified Lord in communion. Christ's words at the Last Supper were prefaced by an invitation to communicate. Before He presented His separated body and blood, the Lord said: "Take, eat . . . Drink ye all of this." Whatever the variants in the Gospel transmission of Christ's words, they indicate an indissoluble connexion between communion and the memorial of the sacrifice. Communion should therefore always be part of the eucharistic action, because it is by that action as a whole that the memorial of the sacrifice of the cross is made and we are united to the heavenly intercession of Christ and share in His real presence, by partaking of His body and blood offered on our behalf to the Father.

Thus the Church, in the Eucharist, accomplishes the memorial of Christ, presents His sacrifice to the Father, shares in His heavenly intercession, "proclaims the Lord's death until He come", in the thanksgiving of the whole eucharistic prayer, which recalls the work of redemption; in the breaking of the bread, which is the body of Christ given for us; in the raising of the cup containing the outpoured wine, which is the blood of Christ, of the new covenant, shed for us for remission of sins; by presenting on the altar the separated body and blood of Christ as in the sacrifice on the cross; by taking, eating, and drinking the eucharistic elements in the act of communion. In a single eucharistic action which comprises the Word of God (lections), praise (psalms and responses), prayer (petitions and intercession), the Church's offering (offertory), thanksgiving (the eucharistic prayer), and communion (from the Lord's prayer to the blessing), the liturgy presents the sacrifice of the cross and unites us to the heavenly intercession, until the Lord's return. So the Church performs the memorial of the Lord in a liturgical act which is a perfect unity; it is obedient to His command: "Do this as the memorial of me"; it proclaims the Lord's death until He comes.

THE PROCLAMATION OF THE CROSS

Attention must be finally given to St. Paul's statement at the end of his account of the Last Supper: "For as often as ye eat this bread, and drink the cup, ye proclaim the Lord's death till he come" (1 Cor. 11:26). St. Paul repeats the "as oft as", ὁσάκις ἐὰν, that he has just used in reference to the cup: "This do, as oft as ye drink it, as the memorial of me. For as oft as . . ." This repetition indicates that St. Paul intends to explain the meaning of the memorial in another way. To do the Eucharist as Christ's memorial and to proclaim His death until He come are expressions which shed light on each other. To proclaim (καταγγέλλειν) can mean to prophesy (Acts 3: 24). So Ignatius says: "Yes, and we love the prophets also, because they too pointed to the Gospel in their preaching and set their hope on Him and awaited Him . . . For the beloved prophets in their preaching pointed to Him."[1] Most frequently the meaning is "to proclaim" with reference to an important event or to the person of Christ. "Being sore troubled because they taught the people, and proclaimed in Jesus the resurrection from the dead" (Acts 4: 2). This proclamation is not a form of teaching but the solemn announcement of a fact or of a person. "Be it known unto you therefore, brethren, that through this man is proclaimed unto you remission of sins . . . This Jesus, whom I proclaim unto you, is the Christ" (Acts 13: 38; 17: 3). The verb is used with the same meaning ten times in Acts and six times in Paul: to proclaim Jesus Christ, the Word of God, the testimony of God, the Gospel, light, faith, the way of salvation, the remission of sins, the resurrection of

[1] *Ad Philad.,* 5, 9.

the dead.[1] The object of this proclamation is always an essential feature of the divine work, when it is not Christ Himself. This solemn proclamation announces the fulfilment of the times, the coming of the days prophesied in the Old Testament (Acts 3: 24), the long-awaited coming of the Messiah (Acts 17: 3), the remission of sins, which is the particular gift of the Messiah (10: 43; 13: 38 f.), and the resurrection of the dead.

The proclamation does not consist in detailed instruction, but is like the announcement of a herald who proclaims a victory or a champion. Nevertheless it relates to something said and not merely to an action; it would therefore be incorrect to suppose that the action of the Eucharist alone is a proclamation of the Lord's death; it is the eucharistic action together with the Word of God that constitutes the proclamation. This proclamation of the death and resurrection of Christ has an eschatological character, since it is the announcement of the new times prophesied in the Old Testament, as St. Paul says in his discourse before Agrippa: "I stand unto this day testifying both to small and great, saying nothing but what the prophets and Moses did say should come; how that the Christ must suffer, and how that he first by the resurrection of the dead should proclaim light both to the people and to the Gentiles" (Acts 26: 22 f.).

It is to be noted that in 1 Cor. 11:26 "to proclaim" is in the indicative and not the imperative and that the apostle is not referring to missionary preaching: only Christians take part in the Eucharist. "Ye proclaim" does not therefore mean "you preach to those outside" (who are absent), but "you perform a solemn proclamation" of the Lord's death, by the Word and the Sacrament. To proclaim the Lord's death means to make present in the eucharistic action, illuminated by the Word of God, the unique event of the redemptive death of Christ, of His sacrifice on the cross. The proclamation of the Lord's death has therefore an essentially liturgical character: through Word and Sacrament the saving event is present.

This liturgical proclamation, which makes salvation present, is to be understood in the light of the proclamation at the Passover: "It is because of that which the Lord did for me when I came forth out of Egypt" (Ex. 13: 8). It is also to be understood in the light of the

[1] The verb καταγγέλλειν is used eleven times in Acts, but in one instance, 3: 24, it means to prophesy. Elsewhere in Acts and Paul it means a proclamation of salvation (slightly watered down in Acts 16: 21 where Romans are speaking). See J. Schniewind, καταγγέλλω, Th.Wb.NT., I, pp. 69 ff.

liturgical proclamation prescribed in Deuteronomy for the offering of the first-fruits. This is a kind of "eucharistic preface" which sums up the Lord's blessings and accompanies an offering. The believer is to bring the first-fruits of all his crops to the priest and say to him: "I profess (LXX ἀναγγέλλω, I proclaim) this day unto the Lord thy God, that I am come unto the land which the Lord sware unto our fathers for to give us" (26: 3). This preamble is a liturgical proclamation before the Lord. Then, while the priest places the offering before the altar, the believer utters a kind of solemn confession of faith or preface to a thanksgiving: "An Aramean ready to perish was my father . . ." (26: 5-10). This proclamation is a form of thanksgiving to God for His work of redemption, and it is analogous to the proclamation of the Lord's death at the Eucharist, which is both a thanksgiving before God and a making present of the sacrifice of the cross; it is indeed the memorial of the Lord. "By, or at, every celebration of the meal, the Lord's death is proclaimed, not as something that has happened in the past, but as an eschatological event, i.e. as the inauguration of the new covenant. Each Eucharist proclaims the inauguration of the time of the divine salvation."[1]

The eschatological character of the Eucharist is emphasized by St. Paul's concluding words: "until he come". The Synoptic Gospels, with some slight variations, record an eschatological saying of Christ at the Last Supper: "Verily I say unto you, I will no more drink of the fruit of the vine, until that day when I drink it new in the kingdom of God" (Mk. 14: 25; Matt. 26: 29; Lk. 22: 18). And within the same context St. Luke refers to the eschatological banquet: "I appoint unto you a kingdom, even as my Father appointed unto me, that ye may eat and drink at my table in my kingdom; and ye shall sit on thrones judging the twelve tribes of Israel" (22: 29 f.). This eschatological perspective is an integral part of the Eucharist. At the Eucharist Christ appoints a kingdom unto the Church, which participates in it in advance, and in that communion with God which it involves; the Church already sits at table with Christ to eat and drink with Him and enter into communion with Him as in the Kingdom. As through the Eucharist they participate in this communion of the Kingdom and are admitted to the table of Christ, the faithful are assured of their entrance into the Kingdom of God at the Last Day that they may enjoy eternal communion with the Lord. Thus they receive the sign of their belonging to the coming Kingdom at the Eucharist; they are

[1] A. Schlatter, *Paulus, der Bote Jesu*, 1934, p. 325.

given the pledge that they will be able to enter in and have the right to sit at Christ's table "to eat and drink" with Him in eternity.

THE ESCHATOLOGICAL ENTREATY

The Synoptic Gospels record a peculiar saying of Jesus which is a kind of vow: "Verily I say unto you, I will no more drink of the fruit of the vine, until that day when I drink it new in the kingdom of God" (Mk. 14: 25; Matt. 26: 29; Lk. 22: 18). St. Luke provides another saying relating to the Passover which is similar: "With desire I have desired to eat this passover with you before I suffer: for I say unto you, I will not eat it, until it be fulfilled in the kingdom of God" (22: 15 f.). Then Christ took a cup and, having given thanks, He said, "Take this, and divide it among yourselves: for I say unto you, I will not drink from henceforth of the fruit of the vine, until the kingdom of God shall come" (22: 17 f.). The command to take and divide can only mean that Christ Himself did not drink of the cup.[1] According to the Passover ritual the cup was handed round in silence and each one drank; Jesus therefore would have no need to tell His disciples to drink, unless He was breaking with tradition in not drinking Himself.[2] The Lord then declared that He was eating the Passover for the last time; He did not drink of the cup and He made a vow: "I will not drink from henceforth of the fruit of the vine, until the kingdom of God shall come." The use in each passage (four times) of the emphatic negative οὐ μή indicates a solemn oath on the part of Christ, and a further indication of this is the ἀμήν in Mark (14: 25)[3] together with

---

[1] This is agreed by most commentators: T. Zahn, E. Klostermann, A. Schlatter. M. Dibelius, *Jesus*, 1939, p. 114; G. Dix, *The Shape of the Liturgy*, 1945, p. 54.

[2] The same meaning is probably to be attributed to the "Take, eat" in Matthew. By not sharing in the eucharistic communion Christ demonstrated that the fullness of His person was to be found in the bread and the wine and that it was not necessary for Him to eat and drink in order that His disciples might have sacramental communion with Him. The bread and wine were as really His body and blood as His physical being. Hence the saying "With desire I have desired to eat this passover with you" (Lk. 22: 15) is to be understood only of the Passover, which was the setting of the Last Supper.

[3] οὐ μή is found nine times in Mark, on five occasions with ἀμήν, to support an irrevocable promise (9: 1, 41; 10: 15; 13: 30; 14: 25): the bursting in of the power of the Kingdom before the death of certain of the disciples (9: 1; 13: 30), the reward to those who will give a cup of water in the name of Christ (9: 41), the impossibility of entering the Kingdom except as a little child (14: 25). In every case there is a solemn eschatological promise accompanied by "verily, I say . . ."

the λέγω ὑμῖν, I say unto you, which is also found in the Synoptics. This solemn form of oath not to drink the wine is linked in Luke with the command to the disciples to take the cup and divide it *among themselves*. Christ's vow provides the explanation of His unusual action in not drinking the cup: He does not wish to drink wine again until the Kingdom of God shall come.[1]

The question then arises: what is the meaning of Christ's vow not to eat the Passover or to drink wine? The solemn form taken by the vow rules out the idea that it was simply an indication that He was about to die and leave the world. At the time of Jesus vows of abstinence, which played an important role in Judaism, could have three meanings. First, a vow could be made to exercise pressure on someone or to indicate that a decision was irrevocable. So when the Jews plotted against Paul they "bound themselves under a curse, saying that they would neither eat nor drink till they had killed Paul" (Acts 23: 12). Second, a vow of abstinence could be made for more spiritual reasons: to avoid sinning after drink or to mortify the flesh. The Nazirite vow (Num. 6), widely observed at the time of Jesus,[2] had this meaning. A vow in this connexion is a kind of complete consecration to God. There are numerous examples in the New Testament of these vows of consecration, e.g. the devotion to widowhood of the prophetess Anna (Lk. 2: 36 f.), John the Baptist's vow not to eat bread or not to drink wine (Lk. 7: 33; Mk. 1: 6), the acceptance of celibacy (Matt. 19: 12; 1 Cor. 7) or of temporary continence between a husband and his wife (1 Cor. 7: 5). In all these cases, the intention of these vows, whether life-long or for a short period, is that of a special consecration to God for prayer and for the proclamation of the Kingdom. Finally, a vow of abstinence was made as the accompaniment of a prayer that it might be given greater emphasis. Thus a vow, *neder*, εὐχή, came to mean simply a prayer. "For thou, O God, hast heard my vows . . . And unto thee shall the vow be performed. O thou that hearest prayer" (Pss. 61: 5; 65: 1 f.). Saul made the people take a vow of abstinence that God might vouchsafe victory (1 Sam. 14: 24-30); David fasted and lay on the ground to implore God to heal his son (2 Sam. 12: 16).[3]

[1] Jesus refused the wine mingled with myrrh offered Him on the cross (Mk. 15: 23; Matt. 27: 34).

[2] Strack-Billerbeck, II, 748. St. Paul observed this vow for an unknown reason (Acts 18: 18; cf. 21: 23).

[3] The prayer of the sick in James is to be related to the reinforcement of an earnest prayer by fasting: "And the prayer of faith shall save him that is sick, and the Lord shall raise him up" (5: 15). The same word is used here as in connexion

Several passages in the New Testament which connect a vow of abstinence and prayer are to be understood in the same way: ". . . and had prayed with fasting" (Acts 14: 23; 13: 2 f.; Matt. 17: 21; Mk. 9: 29; Lk. 2: 37). The vow of abstinence or fasting is a form of earnest supplication to the Lord: "And I set my face unto the Lord God, to seek by prayer and supplications, with fasting, and sackcloth, and ashes" (Dan. 9: 3; cf. Esther 4: 16; Ps. 109: 24).[1]

In Christ's vow of abstinence at the Last Supper each of these three meanings noted above may be discerned.

First, Christ had taken the decision to suffer the passion for the sake of the Kingdom, and His vow not to take the Passover or wine until the Kingdom had come was a means of engaging Himself in an act of redemptive death that was to be followed by the resurrection and ascension. Christ could not eat of the Passover or drink wine again until the Kingdom had been established.

Second, Christ consecrated Himself wholly to the Father, and His vow of abstinence was a sign of detachment from the world for the glory of God; He belonged only to the coming Kingdom in which the Passover was to be fulfilled. In the high priestly prayer, He said: "And for their sakes I consecrate myself, that they also may be consecrated in truth" (Jn. 17: 19, R.V. margin).

Finally, and this is the most characteristic feature of His vow of abstinence, Christ gave His disciples the symbol of an earnest prayer for the Kingdom. According to the most common meaning of the vow of abstinence, by undertaking not to partake of the Passover or drink wine until the Kingdom of God should come, Jesus was expressing an ardent supplication for the manifestation of the Kingdom. His vow was a concrete form of earnest prayer that the Kingdom of God might come. Following the habitual practice of vows of abstinence He

with St. Paul's Nazirite vow (Acts 18: 18; cf. 21: 23). The word *euche* is used only three times in the New Testament. It would be natural to interpret it in James to mean an earnest prayer, accompanied by a vow and fasting, that healing might take place. The vow of fasting for the healing of the sick was well known in rabbinic tradition (Strack-Billerbeck, IV, 94 ff.), and was in use at the time of Jesus. This agrees closely with the mentality of James, since there is the further statement: "The supplication of a righteous man availeth much in its working" (5: 16). There follows the reference to Elijah and to his earnest prayer for rain, which was accompanied by fasting (5: 17 f.; 1 Kings 17–18: "Get thee up, eat and drink; for there is the sound of abundance of rain" 1 Kings 18: 41).

[1] For the connexion of fasting with the sounding of the trumpets as a memorial to obtain rain see *Taanith*, 3: 3: "In a town which has not received rain . . . there shall be fasting and the sounding of the trumpet."

set a limit to His undertaking: it was to be *until* that Passover was fulfilled in the Kingdom—until the Kingdom should come—until He could drink of the product of the vine in the Kingdom of God His Father. The setting of this limit to the vow is referred to twice, in connexion with the Passover and with the wine, and this is a further indication that Jesus was making a real vow of consecration, of earnest supplication, by His abstinence.[1] The Nazirite vow is expressed as follows: "All the days of his Naziriteship[2] shall he eat nothing that is made of the grape-vine, from the kernels even to the husk. All the days of his vow of Naziriteship[3] there shall no razor come upon his head: until the days be fulfilled, in the which he separateth himself unto the Lord, he shall be holy, he shall let the locks of the hair of his head grow long" (Num. 6: 4 f.). The verbal relationship between the Nazirite vow and Christ's vow of abstinence is immediately obvious. There is the same reference to the product of the vine, the same manner of expressing the extent and limit of the vow, and the same expression of the "fullness" or "fulfilment" of the time fixed for the vow. As the vow comes to an end when the days are fulfilled, so Christ's vow was to come to an end when the Passover was fulfilled in the Kingdom of God.[4] Christ's vow not to eat the Passover nor to drink of the product of the vine is connected with the fulfilment of the Passover in the fullness of the Kingdom. The Passover, which was the sacrament of deliverance, was to be fulfilled when the Kingdom of God was manifested, when the ultimate deliverance had come with the return of Christ. During the period of waiting, the Church makes ready this fulfilment of the Passover and of deliverance in its ministry of the Word and Sacraments.

[1] ἕως, which is used in each of the Synoptic passages, is also used three times in Acts in connexion with the Jewish vow against Paul (23: 12, 14, 21). It translates the Hebrew *ad* which sets the limit of the Nazirite vow (Num. 6: 5; LXX ἕως) and of the vow of abstinence (1 Sam. 14: 24: LXX ἕως). The apocryphal Gospel of the Hebrews records Christ's appearance to James first of all "for James had sworn not to eat of bread from the hour when he had drunk the Lord's cup until (*donec*) he had seen Him risen from the dead" (Jerome, *De vir. ill.*, 2). This is an echo as it were of Christ's own vow and James, in imitation of Jesus, makes his vow a prayer for His resurrection "*donec videret eum resurgentem a dormientibus*, until he should see Him risen from the dead" (*donec* with a final meaning).

[2] R.V. margin.

[3] *Ibid.*

[4] The eschatological character of words derived from πληροῦν, to fulfil, is to be noted.

The Eucharist has indeed a special role to play, since it is the communion in the body and blood of Christ and is the means of present communion in the Kingdom. The Eucharist consecrates now the guests of the eschatological Passover. This fulfilled Passover will simply be a Eucharist at which Christ will visibly preside and in which the faithful of all ages will visibly join. Then Christ will divide afresh this Passover with His disciples who "will eat and drink at His table in His Kingdom". This will be the perfect act of communion, with no veil between the Lord and mankind, on a new earth and beneath new heavens. Until then the Passover must be performed and God must bring the deliverance, of which it is the sacrament, to the fullness of universal salvation. Then cometh the end.

Christ therefore did not declare the promise of the Kingdom by word alone, but by means of a vow of abstinence or an undertaking. He did not drink of the cup and He explained this by means of a vow which postponed the great feast of the eternal Passover until His glorious return. This action has a twofold reference which must be defined.

On the one hand, this vow was an act of earnest prayer that the Kingdom of God might be manifested in its fullness; and by making this vow Christ left an unshakeable assurance to His disciples that the promise of the Kingdom would be accomplished. On the other hand, this vow implies a period of waiting, since it projects the fulfilment of the Passover and the fullness of the Kingdom into the future. And this perspective, of the eternal feast with Christ in His Kingdom, must be preserved in the Church. The Church cannot as yet celebrate that Passover in its fullness, that triumphant feast, that eternal Eucharist at the Lord's table in His Kingdom. The Church waits in hope, while possessing the full assurance that Christ will come again in glory to manifest His Kingdom.

The Church's Eucharist is now, like the Last Supper, an earnest prayer that the Kingdom of God may be manifested and that the Lord may return. In the eucharistic prayer and in this eschatological entreaty, the Church has its unshakeable assurance of Christ's return, because He Himself offered the same prayer for the Kingdom at the Last Supper and reinforced it with a vow. This twofold meaning, eschatological entreaty and eschatological assurance, is to be found in the Aramaic exclamation "*Maranatha*", which may be translated either "*Marana tha*, Lord, come", in which case it is a prayer for His return, or "*Maran atha*, the Lord comes", in which case it is an affirmation of belief in

Christ's return (1 Cor. 16: 22). In the penultimate verse of Revelation there is possibly a translation of the expression, affirming the twofold idea of the certain promise of Christ's return and a prayer that He will return: "He which testifieth these things saith, Yea: I come quickly. Amen: come, Lord Jesus" (22: 20).

When the Church, at the Eucharist, prays earnestly, like Christ, for the manifestation of the Kingdom, of which it has the fullest assurance, it is clearly waiting in hope. The Eucharist as a whole, and every act of worship, should express this waiting and this hope. The Eucharist must not suggest that the Kingdom of God has already been manifested or that the Passover has already reached its fulfilment. The Eucharist must be open to the coming Kingdom.[1] Communion in the body and blood of Christ, which conveys full communion in the Kingdom, conveys it only in a hidden and interior manner, while it intensifies the desire to *see* Christ coming with His saints in glory for the eternal Passover. This power of communion together with this eschatological awareness is clearly expressed in some of the Latin post-communion prayers, e.g. that for Septuagesima in the Roman rite:

> Strengthen, O Lord, Thy faithful by Thy gifts, that by receiving them they may desire them further and that by desiring them they may receive them unto eternity.[2]

The post-communion for the second Sunday after Epiphany reads as follows:

> Vouchsafe, O Lord, so to act in us with a power ever greater that, strengthened by Thy divine sacraments, we may be prepared by Thy grace to receive one day that which they promise.

Having seen how Christ has given the Eucharist an eschatological content and has made it, by His vow of abstinence, an earnest prayer for the fulfilment of the Passover and the coming of the Kingdom, we must now consider once more St. Paul's statement: "For as often as ye eat this bread, and drink the cup, ye proclaim the Lord's death till he come" (1 Cor. 11: 26). "Until he come" ($\overset{\text{''}}{\alpha}\chi\rho\iota\ o\hat{\upsilon}\ \overset{\text{'}}{\epsilon}\lambda\theta\hat{\eta}$) is a phrase in the prospective subjunctive with an idea of finality which is

---

[1] T. F. Torrance, "Liturgy and Apocalypse", *The Annual of the Church Service Society*, May, 1954, pp. 3–18 (French translation in *Verbum Caro*, XI, 1957, No. 41, pp. 28–40).

[2] This prayer is also used as a prayer over the people on the Saturday after Ash Wednesday.

emphasized by the omission of ἄν.[1] It means therefore: "until *at last* he comes; until the goal shall be attained when he will come." In the New Testament, the use of ἄχρι with the aorist subjunctive without ἄν refers to the eschatological goal to be attained: "until (finally) the times of the Gentiles be fulfilled" (Lk. 21: 24; Rom. 11: 25; 1 Cor. 15: 25).[2] The proclamation of the Lord's death "until he come" is therefore in line with Christ's vow of abstinence "until the Passover be fulfilled in the Kingdom of God, until the Kingdom of God come, until the day when Christ shall drink the product of the vine in the Kingdom of God and we shall drink at His table in His Kingdom". Through the eucharistic proclamation, by word and action, like Christ at the Last Supper, the Church prays earnestly for the fulfilment of the Passover and for the coming of the Kingdom of God in glory; this is a prayer which, from earliest times, was expressed by the exclamation: "*Marana tha*, Lord, come."

The proclamation or memorial of the Eucharist is then a prayer for Christ's return. The Eucharist proclaims the death of Christ as the beginning of the last times and presents the memorial of that death to the Father as a prayer for the fulfilling of the times by the return of Christ in glory and by the manifestation of the Kingdom. This is the meaning of the Eucharist according to the *Didache:* "Remember, Lord, Thy Church, to deliver her from all evil, and to perfect her in Thy love, and gather together from the four winds her that is sanctified into Thy Kingdom which Thou didst prepare for her" (10: 5). It is evident that according to this primitive eucharistic prayer the memorial is presented to the Father, on behalf of the Church, and that the Church's primary intention is to offer an eschatological entreaty that God will gather it into the unity of His Kingdom.

The phrase "until he come" expresses the Church's insistent emphasis in the Eucharist, which is similar to that of Christ, expressed in His vow "until the Kingdom of God shall come". The Eucharist is the Church's most earnest entreaty for the return of Christ and for the coming of the Kingdom. In this earnest prayer all acts of intercession are gathered together, for the return of Christ is the summing up of all

[1] F. Blass and A. Debrunner, *Grammatik des neutestamentlichen Griechisch*, 1949, 383: 2, p. 168.

[2] See also Acts 3: 21 ("until the times of restoration of all things"), Phil. 1: 6 ("until the day of Jesus Christ") and Rev. 17: 17 ("until the words of God should be accomplished"). There is here the same idea of eschatological fulfilment. In nine of the eighteen passages in the New Testament where ἄχρι is used, with a verb or noun, it has this eschatological reference.

prayers and the ultimate answer to them all. When the Church intercedes for the faithful and for mankind, it is that they may be ready to receive the Lord when He comes, that they may be introduced into the communion of the coming Kingdom. Just as "this gospel of the kingdom shall be preached in the whole world for a testimony unto all the nations; and then shall the end come" (Matt. 24: 14), so, by the Eucharist, the Church "proclaims the Lord's death until the attainment of the goal when He returns". It prays to the Father with such earnestness, and presents to Him the Son's intercession on the cross and in heaven, and unites itself to that intercession in order that He may fulfil the Passover and manifest His Kingdom by the glorious return of Christ. The Eucharist is entirely orientated in this eschatological direction, towards the fulfilment of the Passover and of the Kingdom, for which all the faithful will be raised. The worship of the new covenant, like that of the old, is stretched out towards this ultimate fullness in the Kingdom, as Paul stated to Agrippa: "And now I stand here to be judged for the hope of the promise made of God unto our fathers; unto which promise our twelve tribes, earnestly serving God night and day, hope to attain" (Acts 26: 6 f.).

As it celebrates the Eucharist, the Church is like the intercessory angels or Watchers of Isaiah's vision (62: 6 f.) which call Yahweh to remembrance that He may restore Jerusalem in glory.

As it celebrates the Eucharist, the Church, like the angelic Watchers, never ceases to call the Lord to remembrance of His promise of the Kingdom; it has no respite in its earnest prayer and allows none to God until He restores Jerusalem, setting it up in glory in the midst of the earth, until Christ comes and the eternal Passover is fulfilled in the eternal Kingdom. Until Christ finally comes, the Church presents His death as a memorial before the Father.

We can thus understand the joy and confidence of the Church, when it celebrates the Eucharist. The Lord has provided in it the means of meeting Him and discovering the communion of the Kingdom. The Church cannot but wish to celebrate it frequently, when it knows that, through it, it really receives the Lord and attains the Kingdom which is to come, and when it knows that, through it, its prayer becomes that of the Son before the Father and hastens the coming of the Day of God. Christ desired greatly to eat the Passover with His disciples, and the Church also desires greatly to communicate with Him in the Eucharist, and to eat and drink one day at His table in His Kingdom, when His vow will be fully granted by the fulfilment of the

Passover. Since the Church's liturgy is stretched out towards this coming fulfilment, it finds its greatest joy in the Eucharist, by means of which it attains its Lord and the Kingdom, in the mystery of the signs, by praying the Father earnestly for the return of Christ and the coming of the Kingdom in a glory that will be visible.

III

THE EUCHARISTIC SACRIFICE

It is possible to speak of the Eucharist as a sacrifice within the context of the biblical conception of the memorial.

The Eucharist is a sacrifice for three reasons:

1. It is the sacramental *presence* of the sacrifice of the cross, by the power of the Holy Spirit and the Word, and it is the liturgical *presentation* of the Son's sacrifice by the Church to the Father, in thanksgiving for all His blessings and in intercession that He may grant them afresh.

2. It is the *participation* of the Church in the intercession of the Son before the Father in the Holy Spirit, that salvation may be accorded to all men and that the Kingdom may come in glory.

3. It is the *offering* which the Church makes of itself to the Father, united to the Son's intercession, as its supreme act of adoration and its perfect consecration in the Holy Spirit.

This sacrificial understanding of the Eucharist, in the light of the biblical memorial, provides a basis for a Christian definition of sacrifice:[1] *sacrifice is an act of presentation of a reality to God, for the purpose of a blessing upon that reality or upon him who presents it.*

Thus, in the early Church, *sacrificium* denoted not only the expiatory sacrifice of Christ but everything offered to God—the offertory at the Eucharist, the Eucharist as a whole, the eucharistic elements, the spiritual offering (confession of faith, charity, repentance, humility, prayer, fasting) and liturgical offices in general.[2] It has already been seen how the Bible, in its conception of the memorial, provides the basis for these different uses of the sacrificial idea. Whatever the act of

[1] E. Masure, *Le sacrifice du chef*, 1957, pp. 31–51, has attempted a definition in terms of "transference of property" or "return to God" in two stages: surrender and gift. His very broad definition turns sacrifice once more into an action of "humanity before God" (p. 49). It does not seem possible to provide a definition of sacrifice in general and then fit the Eucharist into this category; rather the attempt has been made to start from the biblical memorial and to discover, in the light of this, the meaning of the Eucharist and define Christian sacrifice.

[2] A. Blaise, *Dictionnaire latin-français des auteurs chrétiens*, art. *sacrificium*, pp. 731 f.

sacrifice, it is expressed in Hebrew by the Hiphil of the verb *qarab*, i.e. *hiqrib*, which corresponds in Greek to προσφέρω and in Latin to *offero*, and means to make approach, to present or carry before. Hence at the consecration of the Levites, which is assimilated to an offering, Moses "presents" (*hiqrabta*) them before the Tent of Meeting, before the face of Yahweh, and the children of Israel lay their hands on them and "Aaron shall offer the Levites before the Lord for a wave offering,[1] on the behalf of the children of Israel" (Num. 8: 9-11). The verb generally denotes the act of presentation (Ex. 29: 3; Lev. 1; 2: 12; 8: 21; Num. 7: 2, 10; Hagg. 2: 14; Ezra 8: 35; 1 Chron. 16: 1; 2 Chron. 35: 12, etc.). It expresses the initial and fundamental action, both material and spiritual, of the sacrifice, which consists in *presenting* or bearing before God a being or thing in praise or supplication for the purpose of a blessing. The corresponding Greek and Latin terms (προσφέρω, *offero*) have the same meaning: to bear or carry before. This is the very essence of sacrifice, being its initial and basic movement.

A general definition of sacrifice can be drawn from the Eucharist as a memorial in the biblical sense, and this definition shows that the essential action of Christian worship is at one with basic human nature. Nevertheless the Eucharist as a sacrifice is uniquely original. The offertory, the Church's offering, is an act of presentation of a reality to God for the purpose of a blessing upon that reality. The Church presents the bread and the wine that they may be blessed; it presents the gifts that they may become signs of brotherly charity; it presents itself that it may be sanctified. In this sense, the Eucharist is a sacrifice which resembles those of the old covenant and even those of human beings in general. It is the finest and noblest sacrifice that man has ever offered; it is the sacrifice of praise, which, according to rabbinic tradition, could be offered only in the messianic era. Yet, despite its spiritual character, this sacrifice is primarily a human act which cannot itself claim to please God, in view of the sin and misery of those who offer it. And it is at this point that the complete originality of the eucharistic sacrifice becomes apparent. Christ Himself, through the Holy Spirit and through His Word ("This is my body . . . This is my blood"), makes up what is lacking in the poverty-stricken offering of the Church; He substitutes Himself for the Church's miserable sacrifice.

---

[1] A wave offering was that part of the sacrifice which belonged to the priest; it was waved over the coals of the altar to signify that it was given to Yahweh, and returned by Him to the priest (Ex. 29: 26). The Levites were given as a wave offering to God and so to the people.

In the eucharistic prayer, the Church does not offer a mere human reality; it is enabled to present to the Father, along with its own poverty-stricken offering, the unique and perfect sacrifice of Christ. The glorified Lord takes up into His heavenly intercession the poverty-stricken sacrifice of Christians and it becomes rich with the riches of Christ and acceptable, because carried by the Son into the heavenly sanctuary. The originality, value and effect of the eucharistic sacrifice lie in the fact that through it the Church is able to present a perfect offering, the cross of Christ, which allows access to our offerings, prayers and praises, and makes them acceptable, however poor they may be and however miserable are those who present them.

The term "sacrifice" as a designation of the Eucharist is very important, because it recalls the fact that only the sacrifice of the cross and the heavenly intercession of Christ can make our own sacrifice, thanksgiving and intercession acceptable. Even the expressions "sacrifice of thanksgiving" or "sacrifice of praise" can suggest that our thanksgiving and our praise have some value in themselves, and those who make use of them, for polemical purposes, against the doctrine of the mass, are not always aware that by using them they are in danger of arriving at exactly the opposite conclusion to that which they desire. To avoid or to combat ideas of repetition of or additions to the sacrifice of Christ, they entertain the idea of a Christian sacrifice which is a simple response to the divine gift. But we are not only incapable in ourselves of giving anything of value to God, because of our sin; we are also incapable of responding to His gifts as we should, because of our weakness. God has to give us the will, the joy and the power to thank Him, to pray to Him and to love Him as we should. The Holy Spirit must inspire us to utter praise and He must put upon our lips the Word of God. That is why the Psalms have such an important place in the liturgy. Only Christ can offer a true and acceptable sacrifice, and this is precisely what the Eucharist signifies. When we call the Eucharist a sacrifice, in the sure faith that there is only one true sacrifice, that of Christ, we declare thereby that it is impossible for there to be any acceptable human sacrifice, and that in the Eucharist the Church presents the unique sacrifice of Christ which alone gives meaning and value to our worship and to our charity.

From the sacrificial aspect, the Eucharist is the liturgical presentation of the sacrifice of the Son by the Church to the Father. But the Church can perform this action of presentation only because the sacrifice of the cross is sacramentally present in the Eucharist through the power

78

of the Holy Spirit and the Word. It is this point that must be first considered.

THE SACRAMENT OF THE SACRIFICE

It is evident that the sacrifice of Christ on the cross is alone an expiatory sacrifice. It alone has expiated our sin before God and produced the complete reconciliation of humanity with God; it alone has accomplished the eternal redemption of the faithful by God. From His ascension to His return, Christ presents this redemptive sacrifice in the heavenly sanctuary in intercession, that its effect may be applied to each man. The Eucharist then, which is a sacramental presence of the sacrifice of the cross and a liturgical presentation of that sacrifice to the Father, is not an expiatory sacrifice, but the sacramental means whereby the Father, hearing the joint intercession of the Son and of the Church, applies salvation to all men in order to hasten the manifestation of the Kingdom. Baptism is the decisive beginning of this application, while the Word and the Eucharist continue its completion.

Every expression that may impair the uniqueness of the redemptive sacrifice of the cross and of the heavenly intercession of Christ should be avoided when speaking of the Eucharist, while at the same time the sacrificial reality of the Eucharist must not itself be impaired. This careful balance of the doctrines of mediation and of the sacrament has not always been preserved in theological circles.

Calvin strongly criticized the sacrificial character of the Eucharist, according to the popular medieval idea of repetition, but he affirmed the unity of the sacrifice of the cross and of the Eucharist. "The bread is His *body*. For we have it for this reason, that it may be a covenant in His body, i.e. a *covenant* which has been once for all ratified by the sacrifice of His body, and is now confirmed by eating, viz. when believers eat that sacrifice . . . For the blood was poured out to reconcile us to God, and now we drink it spiritually in order to have a share in that reconciliation. Therefore, in the Supper we have both the covenant and a reinforcing pledge of the covenant."[1]

Calvin saw in the Eucharist, as in the sacrifice of the cross, a ratification of the new covenant with God. By the Eucharist we participate in the reconciliation of the cross and are confirmed in the covenant; the Eucharist includes both the covenant and its renewal in us. The unity of the cross and the Eucharist is thus clearly emphasized; the

[1] See *The First Epistle of Paul the Apostle to the Corinthians*, trans. J. W. Fraser, 1960, pp. 244 ff.

cross is present in the Eucharist as a covenant with God. Calvin, it is to be noted, saw this unity in the act of communion. For him the Eucharist necessarily involved the communion of the faithful by means of which they participate in the reconciliation of the cross, receive the covenant and are confirmed in it. We have already seen that Calvin considered the fraction to be a sign of Christ's sacrifice: "we come to enjoy through it a share in redemption and the application to us of the benefits of His sacrifice . . . the Supper is a mirror which represents Christ crucified to us."[1] But when he saw the sacrifice of the cross in the Eucharist, he always thought of the Eucharist as communion. His opposition to the sacrifice of the mass was largely due to the great number of masses at which there was no act of communion. He would not admit that "by their daily offering the blessing of redemption is brought to the living and the dead" when "a person eats it on his own".[2] But two pages below, speaking of the fraction and the communion, he uses the same terms in order this time to approve of them: "the benefit of the sacrifice is applied to us." There is no doubt that non-communicating attendance at the sacrifice of the mass played a great part in Calvin's criticism of the sacrificial character of the Eucharist. In a sermon of 1558,[3] he gives his interpretation of St. Paul's saying concerning the blessing of the cup (I Cor. 10: 16). It is particularly striking that he upheld the blessing of the cup itself: "For St. Paul does not say that thanks were given with the cup, nor does he say the cup by which blessing is given, but he says that the cup is blessed." This blessing indicates that the cup is "dedicated" to certify to us "that our Lord Jesus Christ gives Himself to us and that the blood which He once shed for our redemption has become the means of our washing and that our stains are purged away by it before God".

Again there is this repeated emphasis upon the unity of the cross and the Eucharist. Christ gives Himself to us, and His blood shed once for all for our redemption thereby becomes the means of our purification before God. Both the redemption of the cross and its present power of purification are certified to us in the Eucharist. The word "certified" is not to be understood simply in its cognitive or intellectual sense; it expresses the certainty of faith which is attached to the reality and presence of Christ and of our purification before God through the mystery of the Eucharist.

[1] *Ibid.*, p. 248.
[2] *Ibid.*, p. 244.
[3] *Sermon 7 on I Corinthians.*

Calvin goes on to define even more clearly participation in the sacrifice of Christ in the Eucharist: "The cup and also the bread must be sanctified in accordance with this practice, in order that the wine may be a figure[1] of the blood of our Lord Jesus Christ and the bread of His body, in order to show that we have truly fed upon Him, and being as it were grafted into Him may have a common life, and that by the virtue of the Holy Spirit may be united to Him,[2] in order that the death and passion that He has undergone may belong to us and that that sacrifice, by which we are reconciled to God, may be attributed and imputed to us now as if we had offered it ourselves in person." By the Eucharist we appropriate the death and passion of Christ, and His sacrifice on the cross, which has reconciled us with the Father, is "attributed and imputed" to us now, as if we had offered it ourselves. The sacrifice of Christ becomes our sacrifice in the Eucharist. The presence of the sacrifice of the cross in the Eucharist could not be better expressed.[3]

The cross is a unique sacrifice in the order of *expiation, reconciliation* and *redemption*. The Eucharist is a sacramental sacrifice in the order of *application* of salvation (remission of sins) based upon the unique expiation, of *communion* based upon the unique reconciliation, and of

---

[1] The word "figure" does not involve a watering down of the idea of the real presence, rather it expresses the outward appearance of the sign and its inner reality, which is the body and blood of Christ. The same word *figura* was used by the Fathers (Tertullian, *Adv. Marc.*, IV, 10: "*Hoc est corpus meum dicendo, id est figura corporis mei*"; Ambrose, *De Sacramen.*, IV. 5.21: "*quod est figura corporis et sanguinis domini nostri Jesu Christi*". For the words *similitudo, figura* and *antitypus* see A. Wilmart, "Transfigurare", *Bull. d'ancienne litt. et d'arch. chrétienne*, I, 1911, p. 280).

[2] Note the demonstrative sense of the sacrament (*to show* that we have truly fed) and the effective sense (we *may have* a common life . . . we *may be united* to Him).

[3] In his *Short Treatise on the Lord's Supper*, Calvin expressed himself more categorically against the idea of sacrifice; but he was criticizing the mass as "a sacrifice for acquiring the remission of sins", in the sense of a repetition of the cross. He accepted the idea of a representation of the sacrifice, as found in the Fathers, but rejected, as Judaic, a form of celebration which recalled only the old covenant. We do not offer or sacrifice, but "we take and eat that which has been offered and sacrificed". He even rejected the idea of the "application of the unique sacrifice" which he was prepared to admit in his *Commentary* on 1 Cor. 11: 24. But the centre of his attack was the mass without communion, which was in danger of appearing to be a repetition of the unique sacrifice of the cross and not a participation in the unique sacrifice and an application of the sacrifice of redemption.

intercession based upon the unique redemption. The Eucharist as the sacrament of the unique sacrifice of the cross applies salvation (remission of sins) to each person, and this was obtained once for all by the expiation of Christ and maintains communion between God and men, which was re-established once for all by the reconciliation of Christ, and unites the intercession of the Church to the heavenly intercession of Christ which was inaugurated once for all by Christ's work of redemption.

Without taking anything from the uniqueness of the cross, the expiation, the reconciliation, or the redemption, the Eucharist is the sacrament or the presence of the unique sacrifice continuing in the Church today the application of salvation and communion with God, together with the intercession of Christ.[1] The Eucharist is the cross present in the Church and extending the unique and perfect work of Christ to all men in space and time and in depth. In the Eucharist, the Church meets Christ who applies salvation to each one, deepens the communion of men with God, intercedes for all and hastens the coming of the Kingdom.

The Eucharist is the sacrament of the real presence of Christ; it is the sacrament of the sacrifice of the cross, "for the Lord does not offer His body to us, just His body with nothing else said about it, but His body as having been sacrificed for us".[2] And the presence of Him that was crucified is not that of an inert victim, but of the Lamb as slain and living in heaven, continually presenting His unique sacrifice in intercession for all men.

The sacramental presence of the sacrifice of the cross is accomplished by the power of the Holy Spirit and of the Word. No action of the

---

[1] The perfecting of the redemption in each one of us through the Eucharist is expressed liturgically in the Latin prayer at the offertory (*secreta*) for the ninth Sunday after Pentecost: "Grant unto us, O Lord, to participate in the mysteries, as is fitting, for each time we celebrate the memorial of the sacrifice (of Christ), the work of our redemption is accomplished (*exercetur*), through Jesus Christ, thy Son, our Lord." *Exercetur* is rich in meaning. It may be rendered "is accomplished", "performs its action" or "is kept in movement"; each translation asserts the permanence and presence of redemption. Cf. O. Casel, "Beiträge zu römischen Orationen. Die Sekret vom 9. Sonntag nach Pfingsten im römischen Messebuch", *Jahrbuch für Lit. Wis.*, XI, 1931, pp. 35 f. Some Protestant eucharistic hymns give clear expression to the presence of the remission of sins in the Eucharist, e.g. *Louange et Prière*, 1957, No. 206: "By the blood that thou hast shed, my sins will be forgiven."

[2] *The First Epistle of Paul the Apostle to the Corinthians*, trans. J. W. Fraser, 1960, p. 248.

Church can be conceived as taking place outside the work of the Holy Spirit, and no liturgy can omit reference to Him. The real presence of Christ and of His sacrifice in the Eucharist is a fruit of His Word: "This is my body . . . This is my blood", but this Word is not a magical formula which produces its effect by recitation. It is the Holy Spirit who gives life to that Word and makes it present in the Sacrament celebrated by the Church. Without the Spirit active within the Church, that Word is a dead letter. A true celebration of the Eucharist is a celebration in the Holy Spirit and in the Church with the Word of Christ. This means that the eucharistic liturgy should include the words of institution and an invocation of the Holy Spirit. Moreover an essential relation must be seen between the liturgy of the Sacrament and the Liturgy of the Word, which together form a unity. The Word of God, proclaimed in the readings and in the preaching, affects the Eucharist, properly so called, through the power of the Spirit. The Word of God, read and preached, acts on the Church through the Spirit and consecrates it to meet Christ in the Sacrament. This consecration is necessary because a Eucharist celebrated by an unworthy community, not consecrated by the Word and the Spirit to discern the Lord's body, would be a scandal and a condemnation of that community. Both the Holy Spirit and the Word are essential to consecrate the Church for the Eucharist. The readings and the sermon are thus integrated with the liturgical action as essential elements. This integration of the Word of God in the eucharistic prayer is strongly emphasized in those prefaces which pick up the theme of the lessons, especially of the Gospel. This relation of Gospel and preface has already been noted, particularly in the Ambrosian rite. A suitable formula of introduction to the biblical readings, in the spirit of this consecration for the Eucharist, would be, for example:

> Come, Holy Spirit of truth:
> Lead us into all truth.
> Lord, consecrate us in the truth:
> Thy Word is the truth (Jn. 16: 13; 17: 17).

THE PRESENTATION OF THE SACRIFICE

The Eucharist is the liturgical presentation of the sacrifice of the Son by the Church to the Father. This is the sense in which we have understood the Eucharist to be a memorial. In Part I of this study, several liturgical types of the Old Testament, such as the *memorial* of the oblation, and the incense, the *presentation* of the shewbread, and the *mercy-seat* by the ark, were considered as symbols of this liturgical presentation.[1] This liturgical presentation is the action of *recalling* to God the Father the sacrifice of God the Son, eternally present, acceptable and effective before Him through God the Holy Spirit; it is the act of *placing* the sacrifice *before* Him, of *stirring up* His pity.

[1] I am in agreement with Douglas Jones ("Anamnesis in the LXX and the Interpretation of I Cor. 11: 25", *J.T.S.*, 1955, VI, pp. 183–91) when he notes the flexibility of the biblical use of the word memorial, *anamnesis* or *mnemosunon*. Nevertheless it does seem to me that he has inadequately related this term to the more general framework of liturgical piety and prayer both in the Old Testament and in Judaism. In particular, he passes too quickly over the case of Cornelius (Acts 10: 4, 31) where the term memorial, *mnemosunon*, is given its full liturgical meaning and has Jewish piety as its context. While I admit the flexibility of the term, it does seem to me that the word, understood in the context of Jewish piety—as in the account of Cornelius—has a quite natural meaning, viz. to recall to God, by an act of praise and prayer, what He has done once for all, and to present what the believer has done as an offering and a prayer.

Douglas Jones seems disturbed by those writers who accord the word "memorial" a primarily sacrificial meaning. In this I am in agreement with him. The twofold meaning of the word must be emphasized, in that it can mean both a recalling to men and a recalling to God, in praise and supplication. When it is applied to the Eucharist, the term means first of all the presence of the divine activity on behalf of His people, as a recalling to the believer, and the presence before God of what He has done in the course of the history of salvation, as a recalling in praise and supplication. The term memorial also has a secondary meaning which refers to the sacrificial understanding of the Eucharist. It does not have this as its primary meaning, but when it is used of the Eucharist it shows how and in what sense it can be conceived as a sacrifice, i.e. only in the sense that it is an act of proclamation, a memorial before men and before God, a presence and an actualization of the unique sacrifice of Christ.

Douglas Jones tends to consider the Passover as no more than a looking backwards, a remembering of the past. But the Passover is an actualization of the work of salvation and in this sense it is an act of proclamation before men and an act of praise, as well as of supplication, before God. As already stated, this understanding of the Passover provides the Eucharist with its proper sacrificial meaning. It would however be a wrong method of approach to affirm first of all, on the basis of an ecclesiastical tradition, that the Eucharist is a sacrifice and then go on to discover a biblical foundation for this. This has not been my line of approach. I began by considering the Eucharist within the context of the Passover and of the memorial, and it was precisely because of this that I was led to a new definition of the conception of sacrifice which is Christian, eucharistic and fully biblical. It is because the Eucharist is the presence of Christ's sacrifice as a memorial that it is a sacrifice at all, but with a new and proper meaning.

Douglas Jones's objection, based upon the danger of seeing the Church's liturgy as an act of mediation, is overcome if the idea of the presence of Christ's work is

The Protestants of the sixteenth century considered that the doctrine of the sacrifice of the mass impaired the uniqueness of the sacrifice of the cross for the remission of sins, and they opposed a popular heresy to the effect that Christ died for original sin while the mass is offered for present sins. Catholic theologians equally opposed this heresy in the *Confutatio pontificia* which was a reply to the Confession of Augsburg.[1] The pontifical theologians expressed the unity of the cross and the mass, and the uniqueness of Christ's sacrifice, in this manner: "He offered Himself once on the cross with the outpouring of blood; He offers Himself now in the mass as in a peaceable and sacramental sacrifice. Once He offered Himself by suffering the passion in a visible form, now He offers Himself in the mass without suffering the passion under the veil of the mysteries."[2] The parallelism and contrast of the words used provides the key to the doctrine of these theologians. On one side, the unique outpouring of the blood, on the other the peaceable and sacramental sacrifice; the reference to the peace offering of the old covenant is to be noted, and this was not a sacrifice for sin, but a communion sacrifice expressing the community of life between the

central in our understanding of the Eucharist. It is not by any act of mediation on the Church's part, offering a new sacrifice, nor by the mediation of the believers' memory, remembering the work of Christ on the cross, that the saving activity is applied now to the people of God and to the world. Just as Christ once for all took the place of every human good work when He *alone* accomplished the work of our salvation, so also in the Eucharist, by the sacramental presence of His unique sacrifice, without any act of mediation by the Church, except for its Word and actions, the Lord takes the place of every liturgical *work* that He may be the only Priest, the only Agent in the Liturgy, in the Church and before the Father. As I have already said, this sacrificial interpretation of the Eucharist as a memorial emphasizes the unique present mediation of Christ, our only Intercessor. It is still His unique work of salvation, His sacrifice on the cross, which is our prayer and praise before God. Neither prayer nor praise are responses possible to the Church on its own, but they are indeed His response which He gave once for all on the cross, and which He continues to give on our behalf and in us to God the Father, in His heavenly intercession, which is sacramentally present in the Eucharist, the memorial of thanksgiving and intercession.

[1] "*Hoc nunquam auditum est a catholicis, jamque rogati plerique constantissime negant ab eis sic doceri.*" *Confutatio pontificia*, II, 3, ed. C. A. Hase, *Libri symbolici Ecclesiae evangelicae*, 1846, pp. LXXIV–LXXVIII. The same refutation appears in *Responsio privata Colcheo-Vesaliensis*, cited by H. Lammer, *Die vortridentinisch-katholische Theologie*, 1958, p. 272.

[2] "*Semel oblatus est in cruce effuso sanguine; hodie offertur in missa ut hostia pacifica et sacramentalis. Tunc offerebatur passibilis in forma visibili, hodie offertur in missa velatus mysteriis impassibiliter.*" *Ibid.*

faithful and God (Lev. 7: 11–16). The term *hostia sacramentalis* also emphasizes the uniqueness of the cross and its sacramental presence in the Eucharist. The adjective "sacramental" applied to the sacrifice expresses, as commonly in theology, the presence of an historical saving event in a mode which is both eschatological and belonging to the Church. It expresses the presence of the salvation accomplished by Christ in the Church His Body, as a hidden anticipation of the Kingdom which is to come. The opposition of terms in the *Confutatio pontificia* is to be understood in this eschatological sense: *in forma visibili*, in a visible form . . . *velatus mysteriis*, under the veil of the mysteries. John Eck, one of the defenders of Catholicism, expressed the same doctrine of sacrifice in this way: "If it may be said that Christ's offering is twofold . . . there is one by which He offered once His living body and His blood to God the Father on the altar of the cross . . .; but there is another, the sacramental offering, by which the Church daily offers Christ through the priests in the sacrifice of the mass . . . as a memorial (*in commemorationem*) . . . of the first offering accomplished once upon the cross."[1] Elsewhere he wrote: "Christ made His offering once on the altar of the cross and its effect flows to us each day."[2] This image of a river, whose source is the cross and which flows to us through the Eucharist, is very suggestive and safeguards both the uniqueness of the sacrifice of the cross and the possibility of a sacramental sacrifice.

The idea of the presentation or showing forth in the Eucharist of the unique sacrifice of Christ is found in certain Catholic theologians of the period between the beginning of the Reformation and the Council of Trent. According to John Eck: "The priest, in the name of the Church (*in persona Ecclesiae*), presents to God the Father the offering accomplished by the Son on the altar of the cross and offers himself."[3] According to John Gropper: "The Church exposes (*proponit*, places before) or re-presents (*repraesentat*) Christ before God the Father."[4] In

---

[1] *Enchiridion*, loc. XVII, 1537, pp. 194 f.

[2] *Ibid.*, p. 196. Cf. the views of numerous Catholic theologians in the sixteenth century, Jean Colchée, A. de Castro, Cajetan, etc. (*D.T.C.*, X, 1, 1104–1109.) Cajetan, *Opuscula*, 1582, II, p. 231, wrote: "The difference is in the mode of offering, for once He offered Himself bodily, now He is offered spiritually. Once He offered Himself in the reality of death, now He is offered in the mystery of death." The same distinction and unity is emphasized by the opposition of the terms *corporaliter . . . spiritualiter, in re . . . in mysterio*.

[3] *Ench.*, loc. XVII, p. 195.

[4] *Antididagma*, 1544, fol. 63, Vº.

view of this one wonders why Catholics and Protestants were unable to agree on this essential aspect of the Eucharist. Calvin could condemn as "a mere quibble" the statement that "the mass is not a new sacrifice, but only an application of the unique sacrifice".[1]

Reformed theologians from the end of the sixteenth century were more willing to consider this proposition, e.g. Philippe du Plessis-Mornay in his treatise *De l'institution, usage et doctrine du saint sacrement de l'Eucharistie, en l'Eglise ancienne*, 1598;[2] Edmé Aubertin, pastor at Paris, in his patristic "summa", *L'Eucharistie de l'ancienne Eglise*, 1633,[3] and above all Pierre du Moulin, minister of the Reformed Church at Paris, in his celebrated *Bouclier de la foi ou défense de la confession de foi des Eglises Réformées du Royaume de France, contre les objections du Sieur Arnoux, Jésuite*, 1635.[4] This book, though apparently concerned with polemics and apologetics, is very ecumenical in what it has to say of the Eucharist. "How and in what sense the Eucharist can be called a Sacrifice", is the title of Section CLVII:[5]

"The Holy Scriptures use the term sacrifice of alms, prayers, a contrite and humble heart, martyrs, ministers of the Gospel, and in general of all sorts of good works. But there are particular reasons for calling the Eucharist a sacrifice:

"I. Because this Sacrament was instituted to proclaim the Lord's death until He come, 1 Cor. 11. Hence the Eucharist may be called a sacrifice, since it represents the sacrifice of the Lord's death. According to the principle that signs and representations ordinarily take the name of that which they signify.

"II. It may be said that in the Eucharist we offer Jesus Christ to God,

---

[1] *Short Treatise on the Lord's Supper* (J. K. S. Reid, *Calvin: Theological Treatises*, 1954, p. 156).

[2] Philippe du Plessis-Mornay was a politician, not a pastor. His work was printed by Jerôme Haultin of La Rochelle.

[3] This was a work of considerable length which surveyed patristic thought in the first six centuries, in reply to Bellarmine, Du Perron and others. It was printed by Pierre Aubert at Geneva and comprises 660 pages plus Index. It indicates the concern of Reformed theologians in former days to base their theology on patristic teaching, which was to them an authoritative guide to the interpretation of the Bible. E. Aubertin is very liberal with regard to the term "sacrifice", much less strict and severe than Calvin and more ecumenical, like all Reformed theologians in the seventeenth century.

[4] This work was also printed by Pierre Aubert at Geneva. For the literature in general see R. Snoeks, *L'argument de tradition dans la controverse eucharistique entre catholiques et réformés français au XVIIe siècle*, 1951.

[5] *Op. cit.*, pp. 629 f.

in so far as we ask God to receive on our behalf the sacrifice of His death.

"III. The Eucharist is a sacrifice of thanksgiving for the divine benefits and especially for the benefit of our redemption through Jesus Christ.

"IV. The early Church had a particular reason for calling the Eucharist a sacrifice, for it was the custom for each believer to bring his gifts and presents to the table, and part of this was used for the Eucharist, while the rest was food for the poor. These presents were called sacrifices and oblations . . ." (There follows a number of patristic quotations.)

"However, there may be two kinds of sacrifice: the one propitiatory and redemptive, the other eucharistic and expressive of thanksgiving. The Eucharist is a propitiatory sacrifice in so far as it is a sacrament and a commemoration, in the same way that the cup is the covenant, the bread is the body of Christ and circumcision was the covenant with God, or as the rock from which the waters flowed was said to be Christ. But strictly speaking, the Eucharist is a sacrifice of thanksgiving; it is, as the canon of the mass states, *sacrificium laudis*, a sacrifice of praise. Hence the Fathers used the term Eucharist i.e. thanksgiving.

"There is no reason to think it strange that one and the same action should be called sacrament and sacrifice. For between a sacrament and a sacrifice there is the same difference as between taking and giving. Thus the Eucharist may be a sacrament in so far as by it God gives us and conveys His grace, and a sacrifice in so far as we offer Him our praise and thanksgiving."

Also worthy of quotation is the conclusion of section CLVIII, "The Belief of the Ancients touching the Sacrifice of the Eucharist". Pierre du Moulin mentions Peter Lombard and Thomas Aquinas and asserts that truth compels both the opponents and upholders of the Reformation to speak in similar terms: "In short, truth is so strong that our opponents, outside the heat of debate, usually say the same things as we do. If you read Lombard, *Sentences*, Book IV, Distinction 12 G, or Thomas Aquinas, *Summa*, Part III, quaest. 83, art. 1, you will see that they are in complete agreement with us and that they maintain that the Eucharist is called a sacrifice solely because a commemoration is made of the sacrifice of the cross and the sacrifice of the Lord's death is applied to us that we may be partakers of its benefit."

The ecumenical spirit of this passage is to be particularly noted, in that it recognizes a general agreement between opposing theologians when they are "outside the heat of debate". Du Moulin then considers that the Eucharist may be called a sacrifice in so far as it is (i) a representation of Christ's sacrifice; (ii) a memorial-offering of Christ to God; (iii) a thanksgiving for redemption and other divine gifts; (iv) the offertory of the Church through the gifts of the believers. The second point is particularly interesting from the pen of a Reformed theologian and it exactly expresses what I have defined by the word "memorial". I should hesitate to use the verb "to offer", and would prefer "to present" so that the expression would not conflict with our contemporary theological language. "It may be said that in the Eucharist we offer (we present) Jesus Christ to God, in so far as we ask God to receive on our behalf the sacrifice of His death." Du Moulin also notes the two kinds of sacrifice: "the one propitiatory and redemptive, the other eucharistic and expressive of thanksgiving." It might have been expected that he would refuse to apply the first to the Eucharist and would accept only the second. But he accepted the term "propitiatory sacrifice" upheld by the Council of Trent: "*Sacrificium visibile esse propitiatorium pro vivis et defunctis.*"[1] For him "the Eucharist is a propitiatory sacrifice in so far as it is a sacrament and a commemoration", i.e. the propitiatory sacrifice of the cross is sacramentally present in the Eucharist under the form of a memorial. The term "sacrament" signifies the actual presence of the propitiatory sacrifice of the cross, and the weaker term "commemoration" no doubt denotes the symbolism of the Eucharist in that it is a rite which figures the sacrifice of Christ. Today we should say that the Eucharist is a sacrifice in so far as it is a sacrament and a symbol, making the sacrifice present sacramentally and representing it symbolically.

Du Moulin then gives some examples: the Eucharist is the sacrament and commemoration of the propitiatory sacrifice in the same way that the cup is in relation to the new covenant, the bread in relation to the body of Christ, circumcision in relation to the old covenant and the rock in the desert to Christ. These examples are not of course to be ranged all on the same level, but they do explain in what sense the Eucharist is to be understood as the sacrament of the propitiatory sacrifice: there is a presence of the reality in the sacrament, in such a way that the sacrament may be said to be the reality which it presents and represents, as the cup *is* the new covenant, and the bread is the body of Christ, circumcision the old covenant and the rock Christ. Finally, du Moulin seems to check himself a little when after all he

[1] *Sessio* XXII, *c.* 2.

expresses a preference for the term "sacrifice of thanksgiving" or "sacrifice of praise" (*sacrificium laudis*). This passage is to be seen as a real ecumenical *tour de force* somewhat hedged in through prudence ("But strictly speaking . . ."). Nevertheless his ideas cannot be denied, and du Moulin has left us a traditional conception of the Eucharist as a sacrament and a sacrifice: a sacrament because in it we take what God gives; a sacrifice because in it we offer our praise and thanksgiving and "offer (present) Jesus Christ to God, in so far as we ask God to receive on our behalf the sacrifice of His death". This is precisely what I mean by "the memorial of thanksgiving and intercession".

In connexion with this understanding of the sacrifice of the cross "proposed, exposed, presented and offered" to the Father in the Eucharist, we may quote a theological poem, written by the seventeenth-century Reformed writer Ogier de Gombaud, who died some time after 1666. This poem is not concerned with the Eucharist, but it shows how the believer, incapable of offering anything of value, takes refuge in the unique sacrifice of Christ and presents it to the Father. Thus although it concerns Christian sacrifice in general, this poem may be applied to the Eucharist, in the spirit of a Philippe du Plessis-Mornay or a Pierre du Moulin:

> Evil subdues me, and so great my woe
> When sin, for all my struggle, wins the day,
> That in this dark abyss I cannot know
> What homage to my Maker I should pay.
>
> I long to offer what thy law commands,
> My prayers, my vows, my fruit of faith to thee,
> But—since my heart deserves not thy demands—
> Christ is my offering, for eternity.
>
> Accept thy Son, O Father: see that cross
> Whereon, to pay the utmost that I owe,
> In blood and death He yields thee all His loss;
>
> And by His love's abundance I implore
> No longer, Lord, thy right of justice show,
> But shed thy pity, now and evermore.[1]

In the eighteenth century, in an attempt to further unity with the

---

[1] Quoted by A. M. Schmidt, "Les poètes calvinistes français des origines à la révocation de l'édit de Nantes, témoins d'une vie théologique", *Revue Réformée*, IV, 1950, pp. 274 f.

Church of England, Father Le Courrayer published a *Dissertation sur la validité des ordinations des Anglais et sur la succession des évêques de l'Eglise anglicane*.[1] He was attacked for his ecumenical zeal and so, in 1725, he issued a *Défense de la Dissertation sur la validité des ordinations des Anglais*. It must be acknowledged that he was mistaken in separating the doctrine of the eucharistic sacrifice from that of the real presence and in affirming that Catholics and Anglicans could agree on the first without being united on the second. Nevertheless his conception of sacrifice is very interesting, in that he wished to be faithful to Trent and at the same time shared the conception of those seventeenth-century Reformed theologians whose works have been quoted. "The Council", he says, "calls the celebration of the Eucharist a sacrifice, *ut Ecclesiae relinqueret sacrificium*, because, since the sacrifice consists in the offering of a sacrificed victim and since the passion of Christ is always present, every time that this victim is offered, the sacrifice of Jesus Christ is offered. ... But the sacrifice is not renewed, for Jesus Christ dies only once. Nor is it a sacrifice which is continued or supplemented, since it had its perfection and completeness in the death of Christ. It is rather a sacrifice which is represented, *quo cruentum illud semel in cruce peragendum repraesentaretur;* a sacrifice recalled, *ejusque memoria in finem usque saeculi permaneret;* and a sacrifice applied, *atque illius salutaris virtus applicaretur.* There is therefore in the Eucharist a true sacrifice, in the sense that there is therein made to God *the oblation of a death which is always present, mortem annuntiabitis.* But as this death is not repeated, this sacrifice is no more than the representation of another one, *Hoc facite in meam commemorationem* ... There is no question here of simply recalling Christ's death to remembrance, but of the offering of that remembrance to God in order that in virtue of what He has suffered He may have pity upon us."[2]

Father Le Courrayer was rightly criticized for separating the doctrine of the eucharistic sacrifice from that of the real presence, but his understanding of the sacrifice as a memorial-offering is quite in line with the biblical concept of the memorial, as well as with the thought of du Moulin, and therefore has a place in any ecumenical discussion of the Eucharist. His views have been quoted here to show that when Protestants and Catholics, like du Moulin and Le Courrayer, seek to re-think the doctrine of the eucharistic sacrifice in an ecumenical context, they reach positions which are very close to each other.

[1] Published in French at Nancy in 1723.
[2] *Op. cit.,* IV, c. 4, pp. 157 f.

THE SACRIFICE OF THANKSGIVING

Having defined the connexion between the liturgical presentation of the sacrifice of the Son by the Church to the Father and the unique sacrifice of the Son on the cross, we must now consider the primary meaning of this liturgical presentation, which is a thanksgiving for the divine blessings and especially for redemption in Jesus Christ. Tradition is unanimous that the Eucharist is a sacrifice of thanksgiving or praise. According to Justin: "The offering of fine flour, which was prescribed to be presented on behalf of those purified from leprosy, was a type of the bread of the Eucharist, the celebration of which our Lord Jesus Christ prescribed, as a memorial of the passion which He endured on behalf of those who are purified in soul from all iniquity, in order that we may at the same time thank God for having created the world, with all things therein, for the sake of man, and for delivering us from the evil in which we were, and for utterly overthrowing principalities and powers by Him who suffered according to His will."[1] Irenaeus, writing a little later, expresses the same idea: "It behoves us to make an offering to God, and in all things to be found grateful to God our Creator, in a pure mind, and in faith without hypocrisy, in well-grounded hope, in fervent love, offering the first fruits of His own created things. And the Church alone offers this pure oblation to the Creator, offering to Him, with giving of thanks, the things taken from His creation. . . . It is therefore also His will that we, too, should offer a gift at the altar, frequently and without intermission. The altar then is in heaven, for towards that place are our prayers and offerings directed."[2]

Very many other patristic passages could be quoted in the same vein, for this was a continuous tradition.[3] At the Reformation the expression "sacrifice of praise" was accepted also by Luther, who wrote in 1530: "The offering of the bread and the wine is also a sacrifice of praise. This Christian sacrifice is not to reconcile us with God, but these are the gifts bestowed by God on those who are reconciled."[4] Elsewhere he violently criticized the sacrifice of the mass[5] but he preserved the idea of the sacrifice of thanksgiving.[6]

[1] *Dial. cum Tryph.*, 41.   [2] *Adv. Haer.*, IV, 18: 4, 6.
[3] See J. Juglar, *Le sacrifice de louange*, 1953.
[4] Cf. *In Deo omnia unum*, Festgabe für Fr. Heiler, p. 290.
[5] Weimar-Ausgabe, VIII, p. 493.
[6] V. Warnack, "Das Messopfer als ökumenisches Anliegen", *Liturgie und Mönchtum*, XVII, 1955, pp. 65 ff.; R. Prenter, "Das Augsburgische Bekenntnis und die römische Messopferlehre", *Kerygma und Dogma*, I, 1955, pp. 42 ff.

Similarly Calvin, having criticized the mass as a sacrifice "for purchasing the forgiveness of sins, propitiating God or obtaining justification",[1] shows that the whole of the Christian life is a sacrifice of thanksgiving and writes of the Eucharist in particular: "This kind of sacrifice is indispensable in the Lord's Supper, in which, while we show forth His death, and give Him thanks, we offer nothing but the sacrifice of praise. From this office of sacrificing, all Christians are called 'a royal priesthood', because by Christ we offer that sacrifice of praise of which the apostle speaks, the fruit of our lips, giving thanks to His name (1 Peter 2: 9; Heb. 13: 15). We do not appear without gifts in the presence of God without an intercessor. Christ is our Mediator, by whose intervention we offer ourselves and our all to the Father; He is our High Priest, who, having entered into the temple on high, opens up a way of approach for us; He the altar on which we lay our gifts, that whatever we attempt, we may attempt in Him; He it is, I say, who 'hath made us kings and priests' unto God and His Father" (Rev. 1: 6).[2]

This remarkable passage by Calvin emphasizes the sacrifice of praise or thanksgiving and includes in it the idea of an offering in Christ the Intercessor: "He is our altar on which we lay our gifts, that whatever we attempt, we may attempt in Him." The Reformers did not speak of the Eucharist as a sacrifice in order to recognize in it thereafter the different kinds of sacrifice—thanksgiving, intercession etc. They first defined the Eucharist as a sacrifice of thanksgiving or praise, in which they included prayer and the Church's offering, as so many oblations placed upon the altar of Christ the Intercessor in the movement of thanksgiving. This insistence upon the sacrifice of praise, together with the criticism of the mass as a sacrifice for the remission of sins, compelled the Council of Trent to be precise in its definitions, to such an extent that agreement was made more difficult.

THE SACRIFICE OF INTERCESSION

The agreement of both Catholics and Protestants, that the Eucharist is a sacrifice of praise or thanksgiving, has now been noted. A further aspect of the Eucharist, as a sacrifice of intercession, that God may now grant the very blessings for which He is praised, presents greater difficulties, and these difficulties arise from three basic causes:

1. The theologians of the fourteenth and fifteenth centuries had laid

[1] *Inst.*, IV. xviii. 14.
[2] *Ibid.*, 17.

particular stress upon the relation of the Church to the sacrifice. They laid no stress upon the fact that it is Christ who presents Himself to the Father in intercession. Consequently a division arose between the sacrifice of the cross and that of the altar, and the latter became a repetition of the former. Such a belief seemed to be in contradiction to the teaching of Hebrews and to impair the doctrine of the uniqueness of the expiation upon the cross.

2. Non-communicating attendance, private masses and votive masses *pro vivis et defunctis*, had issued in a doctrine of the efficacy of the eucharistic sacrifice *ex opere operato:* the mass produced a propitiatory effect independent of the act of communion or even of the presence of believers and it could be offered on behalf of the departed. This conception contributed to the assimilation of the mass to the expiatory sacrifice of the cross which was itself efficacious *ex opere operato*, since Christ was alone on Calvary.

3. Catholic theology had perhaps laid too great an emphasis upon the propitiatory character of the mass as a sacrifice for the remission of sins, as a means of reconciliation with God and of obtaining justification. In this, as in connexion with the former points, the Reformers saw a scandalous repetition of the one expiatory sacrifice of the cross.

With regard to the first point, it is clear that the Reformers' cry of alarm had its effect and that, even before the Council of Trent, Catholic theologians were emphasizing the unity of the eucharistic sacrifice and the sacrifice of the cross, there being one offering of Christ under two different modes: "By the commemoration, the unique and only oblation is made, which was accomplished by Christ once for all on the cross," writes Jean Colchée.[1] Later, Ruard Tapper and Guillaume Lindanus, of Louvain, used the idea of the heavenly sacrifice to emphasize the unity of the Eucharist and the perpetual sacrifice of Christ begun upon the cross.[2] In the seventeenth century, following this same line, which was also that of Bossuet, Denys Amelote wrote very clearly: "If the Son of God offers His blood as a victim for us in heaven, and if He offers it by interceding for our salvation, He does not take anything away from His sacrifice on the cross, by offering Himself since His death, but he represents the price to His Father for those who approach Him through His mediation. Why then cannot He, who remains with His Church day by day unto the end of the ages and makes His body and His blood present under the signs of

[1] *Quadruplex concordiae ratio* Ia p.: De missa, n. 9, 1544.
[2] R. Tapper, *Declaratio articulorum*, 1554; G. Lindanus, *Panoplia evangelica*, 1559.

bread and wine, be offered to God, by Himself as High Priest and by the priests as His ministers, to renew for us the memory of His passion and to communicate to us its merits?"[1] This concern to assert the complete unity of the eucharistic sacrifice and the sacrifice of the cross with the heavenly intercession is certainly one of the fruits of the Reformation.

With regard to the second point, the Reformers showed themselves to be equally adamant. Since they believed in the real presence and its efficacy in the communion, they could not admit that the eucharistic sacrifice produced fruits *ex opere operato*, independently of communion or of the presence of the faithful, *pro vivis et defunctis*. The Catholic theologians of the *Confutatio pontificia* avoided the expression *ex opere operato* in relation to the efficacy of the sacrifice, and John Eck, in a letter to Melanchthon of August 27, 1530, refused to commit the Church on this point.[2] Moreover the attempt was made to show that the application of the sacrifice of the cross to the faithful at the Eucharist is not automatic but requires the faith and charity of those present.[3] Nevertheless it does benefit the faithful departed, who are members of the Body of Christ.[4] But here we encounter the question of prayer for the dead, which is a different problem.

With regard to the third point, the Reformers wished to reserve to the sacrifice of the cross alone all expiatory virtue. Melanchthon distinguished two kinds of sacrifice: the propitiatory sacrifice, appeasing the wrath of God and securing remission of sins, offered only by Christ on the cross, and the eucharistic sacrifice to thank God for His benefits offered by the faithful who have been reconciled.[5] The Confession of Augsburg condemned "the abominable error that our Lord Jesus Christ, by His death, expiated only original sin and that He instituted the mass to be a sacrifice for other sins. He would thus have made the mass a sacrifice for the living and for the dead, intended to remove their sin and reconcile them to God."[6]

This view may have been given currency in popular preaching, but, as seen above, it was rejected as contrary to Catholic dogma by theologians in authority. Later, the Confession of Augsburg contrasts

---

[1] *Abrégé de théologie*, 1675, *1.* VI, *c.* 40.
[2] *Corpus Reformatorum*, II, col. 317.
[3] *D.T.C.*, X. i, col. 1106.
[4] J. Eck, *Enchiridion*, XXXVIII, p. 407.
[5] *Apologia Confessionis*, XXIV, 19.
[6] Art. XXIV, "Of the Mass".

the doctrine of the mass with justification by faith. Here again, as noted above, Catholic theologians declared that the application of the sacrifice is not automatic, and that it requires faith and charity, by means of which the Church is directed to the unique sacrifice of Christ, which is the source of justification. Yet, even if Protestant polemic was directed against positions which, from the point of view of strict Catholic theology, were not accepted as orthodox, it is quite clear that it was justified by popular preaching and practice which laid emphasis upon the mass as a sacrifice for the sins of the living and the dead, and, by this emphasis, compromised belief in the unique expiatory sacrifice of Christ, which is the source of justification.

The Council of Trent attempted to settle the question of the sacrifice of the mass, and its statement requires careful consideration.

"If anyone says that the sacrifice of the mass is only a sacrifice of praise and thanksgiving or a simple commemoration of the sacrifice accomplished on the cross, and not rather a propitiatory sacrifice, let him be anathema."[1]

According to the Council, the Eucharist is not just a sacrifice of praise and of thanksgiving; it is not a simple commemoration; it is also a propitiatory sacrifice (*propitiatorium*). It is to be noted at the outset that although the Council declares itself against those Protestants who will admit only the sacrifice of praise or the simple commemoration, it equally condemns the "Catholic" error, stigmatized in the Confession of Augsburg, to the effect that the mass has an expiatory effect for present sins, while the cross was the expiation of original sin. Indeed to choose the adjective "propitiatory" is to avoid "expiatory", which would have created a confusion between the mass and the cross. Expiation suggests the passion and the death, while propitiation may be understood to refer to the memorial of the unique expiatory sacrifice, which is a memorial presented to the Father as a plea for His grace.[2] Even if "propitiatory" may shock a Protestant, it is to be noted that this adjective avoids any idea of present expiation, in terms of the cross, or present redemption in terms of the unique sacrifice of Christ.

The root of the Old Testament word translated "propitiation" is K P R, and denotes originally "to cover". Propitiation consists in the fact that God covers our sins in order to see them no more, or that the priest of the old covenant "covered" or sprinkled a sacrifice with

[1] *Sessio* XXII, *c.* 3.
[2] M. Lepin, *L'idée du sacrifice de la messe d'après les théologiens depuis l'origine jusqu'à nos jours*, 1926, p. 328.

blood. Thus in the rite of the Day of Atonement the High Priest sprinkled, with the blood of the sin offering, the mercy-seat, the *kapporeth*, the "covering" of gold, which "covered" the ark, and where Yahweh manifested Himself between the two golden cherubims (Lev. 16: 14; Ex. 25: 17-22). Propitiation, according to the Old Testament, consists in sprinkling the blood which comes from the sin offering. Hence "propitiation" may denote the presentation of the blood of a sacrifice which has been performed elsewhere. The Eucharist, as a "propitiation", is the presentation of the blood of the sacrifice of the cross, in intercession before God, on the altar, which is a new mercy-seat where God manifests Himself to His people, the Church.

The word "propitiation" also involves the idea of making someone propitious by imploring him to have mercy. This act of imploring can be considered as a request for the forgiveness of sins, but it can also be seen as an intercession for the needs of men. *"Kyrie eleison"*—Have mercy, Lord—can be said after a confession of sin, but it can also be used, as in the liturgy, as a response to a litany which is a form of general intercession. To ask for mercy is not just to ask for forgiveness, it is also to ask for the grace and blessing of God. Catholic theology has laid too much emphasis upon propitiation for sin in the mass, and this can lead to a confusion with the sacrifice of the cross, and hence the legitimate fear of Protestants who wish to remain obedient to the teaching of Hebrews: "there is no more offering for sin" (10: 18). It has been seen how and within what limits Pierre du Moulin was prepared to accept the expression "propitiatory sacrifice", as applied to the Eucharist, "as a sacrament and commemoration". There is no doubt that an ecumenical agreement could have been reached on the basis of a wider formula than that of "propitiatory sacrifice", interpreted too narrowly as a sacrifice for sin. The understanding of "propitiation" in the sense of "presentation" or "intercession" would have avoided the confusion of the sacrifice of the Eucharist with the sacrifice of the cross.

The Council of Trent clearly defined the relation between the mass and the cross, but it is regrettable that the adjective "propitiatory" should have been interpreted almost exclusively in terms of a petition for forgiveness. Canon 3 is further explained in Chapter 2 of Session XXII:

"And, since in this divine sacrifice which is accomplished in the mass, the same Christ is contained and immolated in a bloodless manner, who *offered Himself once for all* on the altar of the cross in a bloody manner (Heb. 9: 27): the holy Council teaches that this sacrifice is truly propitiatory (Can. 3), and that through it it is brought about, if we approach God with a sincere heart and a right faith, with fear and respect, both contrite and repentant, that *we obtain mercy and we find grace to help us in time of need* (Heb. 4: 16). Because, prevailed upon by this oblation, the Lord, when He accords us grace and the gift of repentance, remits our faults and our sins, even the greatest of them. It is indeed one and the same sacrifice, and the same one offers it now through the ministry of the priests who once offered it Himself on the cross; the only difference lies in the manner of the offering. The fruits of this (bloody) oblation are abundantly received by means of the non-bloody oblation, in such a way that the first is in no way at all impaired by the second (Can. 4). That is why, in accordance with the tradition of the Apostles, it is offered not only for the sins of living believers, for their penalties, satisfaction and other necessities, but also for the departed in Christ who are not yet completely purified."

Notice must first be taken of the insistence in this Chapter on the unity of the Eucharist and the cross. It is already stressed in Chapter 1: "(the Eucharist), a visible sacrifice which is a fitting representation of the bloody sacrifice accomplished once for all on the cross, to extend the memorial unto the end of the ages, and so to apply its saving power for the forgiveness of our daily sins." Notice should also be taken of the spiritual conditions laid down to receive grace through the sacrifice, and these conditions prevent a false interpretation of the efficacy of the sacrifice, *ex opere operato*, as if it were an automatic action. In addition to these subjective conditions, the Council also added some objective ones: grace and the gift of repentance. This insertion was lacking in the text of September 5, 1562. Its intention is to assign a place to the efficacy of the sacrament within the normal economy of justification. The eucharistic sacrifice does not act directly of itself, but within the order of grace and in connexion with the divine gift of repentance. It may be said that by the eucharistic sacrifice the Church pleads for mercy and grace, that God grants this grace and the gift of repentance and, by means of these, the forgiveness of sins. But the granting of these is dependent upon certain spiritual conditions— sincerity and faith, fear and respect, humility and the confession of sins.

In this instance the Council of Trent anticipated Protestant criticism, expressed for example in the *Confessio Augustana*, that the sacrifice of the mass by which sins are remitted *ex opere operato* conflicts with justification by faith; indeed the eucharistic sacrifice and its efficacy are assigned a place within the economy of grace and justification.

The eucharistic sacrifice is a sacrifice of thanksgiving and intercession. This intercession, which is the presentation of the Son's sacrifice by the Church to the Father, pleads for the divine grace for all the needs of men: the forgiveness of sins by the application of the unique expiation to each individual, the gifts of faith, hope and charity, the blessing of the Lord upon all things, the hearing and granting of all the requests made by each person in the liturgy.

It has been seen that the Reformed theologians of the seventeenth century, like Pierre du Moulin, understood the biblical and traditional meaning of the "eucharistic and propitiatory" sacrifice and were therefore able to express an integrated and ecumenical theology. A further passage from Philippe du Plessis-Mornay may be quoted to show both the extent and limitation of the Reformed understanding of post-Tridentine Catholic theology in relation to the Eucharist as a sacrifice:

"Nevertheless it needs to be considered as in some sense a sacrifice, in so far as it is the commemoration of the propitiatory sacrifice of our Lord on the cross, in accordance with the saying, Do this in remembrance of me; you proclaim the death of the Lord until he come. So that as the Lamb was, after a fashion, a propitiatory sacrifice, in so far as it prefigured Christ's sacrifice, the Eucharist also may be called the same, in so far as it recalls it to us and represents Him to us crucified before the eyes of our faith. But another sacrifice issues from this commemoration, a true sacrifice of praise and thanksgiving which the Church calls the Eucharist. When we remember that God has so loved the world, or rather the Church hated by the world, that He has given His dear eternal Son for mortal men, the righteous for criminals, to the ignominious death of the Cross, to redeem them from their sins, we worship the bowels of His mercy . . . And this faith applies the sacrifice to us, making it personal . . . (So we can say: I am sacrificed with Christ, I live, yet not I, but Christ in me.) What can we do less than to give ourselves, to sacrifice ourselves to Him? To present to Him, as the Apostle says, our bodies a living sacrifice, holy, acceptable to God, which is our reasonable service? . . . And the commemoration of this propitiatory sacrifice can be called, even if inaccurately, a sacrifice.

"(Thanksgiving issues in a gift of self.) Here we have another sacrifice; a peaceable sacrifice in so far as peace is established between God and the faithful believer, a sacrifice of praise, in so far as every success is given us in God and God Himself in this peace. In short there is a sacrifice of ourselves in the Eucharist through thanksgiving.

"It was for reasons such as these that the Fathers sometimes called the Eucharist a sacrifice or a commemorative sacrifice and a sacrifice of thanksgiving on the part of the faithful. If our opponents were satisfied with this, we should not dispute nor should we reject the word sacrifice. But if they tell us that the mass is a propitiatory sacrifice, for the living and the dead, we must tell them that they must declare whether they base the mass on the Last Supper or whether they find its institution elsewhere."[1]

Philippe du Plessis-Mornay's reticence derives from the conception that the Roman mass is a propitiation *pro vivis et defunctis*, distinct from communion and even attendance at the Eucharist. This is the same reaction already noted on the part of the sixteenth-century Reformers. It is precisely this that raises a difficulty for du Plessis-Mornay, since he can write further on, in terms which are very close to those of Tridentine theology: "So we do not, according to St. Cyprian, offer Jesus Christ Himself; but we offer His passion, we offer Him already immolated on the cross; we commemorate His death; we represent it to God for the remission of our sins."[2]

This doctrine of the *representation* to God of the death of Christ for the remission of sins is, in my view, precisely what the Council of Trent wished to express by its idea of the propitiatory eucharistic sacrifice. It would also be proper to criticize du Plessis-Mornay for too exclusive an insistence upon the remission of sins in his doctrine of the propitiatory eucharistic sacrifice. He expresses the same idea later in his treatise: "We represent to God as a propitiation for our sins Christ who died for our redemption."[3] Here the unity of the Eucharist and the cross, as well as their distinction, are clearly expressed; *Christ died for our redemption;* the Eucharist is the *representation of the cross to God as a propitiation for our sins.* There is no need to insist further that by "represent" is not meant "imitate" but "to present afresh" (in the sacramental and liturgical sense), "to re-present".

Another Reformed writer of the seventeenth century, Jacques Basnage (1653–1723), has also formulated very explicitly this doctrine of

---

[1] *De l'institution, usage et doctrine du saint sacrament de l'Eucharistie, en l'Eglise ancienne*, 1598, III, ch. I, pp. 353 ff.

[2] *Ibid.*, p. 539.

[3] *Ibid.*, p. 556.

the eucharistic sacrifice and connected it with the fraction and with the wine outpoured: "In the Eucharist it is not just a matter of the priest and the communicant remembering the sufferings of Jesus, recalled by the sight of the bread broken and the wine outpoured, but also the bread and wine are offered to God that He may remember the same sufferings of His Son and that, touched by the sacrifice of the cross, He may be appeased and may grant the remission of sins. There is no new sacrifice, but a commemoration of the sacrifice of the Son of God who, being represented to His Father by the symbols of bread and wine, constrains Him to let Himself be touched and to grant us the fruits of the true sacrifice which is that of the cross."[1] Even though it be necessary to level at this the same criticism to which du Plessis-Mornay is exposed, the statement that the sacrament "constrains Him to let Himself be touched" is worthy of note. Certain modern Reformed theologians may hesitate to accept so clear a doctrine,[2] but where exactly does Reformed tradition find its expression?

THE EUCHARISTIC SACRIFICE AND JUSTIFICATION BY FAITH

The concern of the Augsburg Confession that the idea of the sacrifice of the mass might impair the doctrine of justification by faith has been already noted. The concern of the Council of Trent to assign a place to the sacrifice of the mass and its efficacy in the economy of justification by faith has also been noted. The same concern is evident in du Plessis-Mornay—"And this faith applies the sacrifice to us, making it personal".

Faith is required on our part for the Eucharist to have its effect. It is not faith which creates the presence of Christ in the Eucharist and makes it a sacrifice of praise. The Eucharist is such because of Christ's promise. Nevertheless faith is necessary and a right intention, in order that the real presence and the eucharistic sacrifice may bear fruit in us. The efficacy of the Eucharist consists in the gift of grace and of repentance, by means of which we bring forth the spiritual fruits of the Eucharist. The Eucharist is therefore active in us under the subjective

---

[1] *Histoire de l'Eglise depuis Jésus-Christ jusqu'à présent*, 1699, p. 995.

[2] Cf. "God makes use of the sacrament, but can it be said that He *is involved* in it? A Calvinistic theologian would always refuse to make such a statement." J. Cadier in *The Reformed and Presbyterian World*, XXV, No. 3, 1958, p. 141. Reformed theologians of the seventeenth century, including Jacques Basnage, did not make such a refusal. How often "Reformed tradition" is invoked and abused to support modern ideas!

conditions of faith and intention and under the objective conditions of the gift of grace and repentance.

One form of Protestant extremism consists in the relegating of salvation to past history, whither we must return by faith, which enables us to reap the benefit of the saving act. This kind of theological thinking often ends in either intellectualism or sentimentality: faith becomes a kind of intellectual or sentimental act of remembering what is past in the history of salvation. The opposite Catholic position attaches itself to the power transmitted to the Church by the Apostles in a former age, a power which is envisaged as making possible the infinite repetition of the redemptive acts. This kind of theological thinking often ends in sacramentalism or automatism. In these two extreme theological positions there is the same idea of salvation as something past, to which a return can be made by faith (Protestants), or which is transmitted by the sacrament (Catholic). A balanced Christian theology supports the view that in Christ the historical act of redemption is made present in faith and in the sacrament. When the Church is united through the Eucharist to the heavenly intercession of Christ, it is united to Him as crucified, and thus makes present the historical act of redemption to apply it to man now, that it may be received in faith and by faith.

In Baptism we are buried now with Christ and we rise in Him. In the Eucharist Christ says to us: "This is my body", and the redemption accomplished on the cross becomes present that it may be applied to us. In the preaching of the Word of God, the Lord says to His servants: "Whoever heareth you, heareth me", and the power of His Word, uttered during His earthly life, is active in the present. In absolution, the living Christ grants the forgiveness of sins for which He died: "Whosesoever sins ye forgive, they are forgiven unto them."

Word and Sacrament make present the fact of historical redemption and apply it to us in faith and by faith.

The doctrine of justification by faith, apart from a conception of present participation in the redemptive work of the living Christ, through Word and Sacrament, issues in a theology of dogmatic purism which is not subject to obedience and cares little for the unity of the Church.

The anti-Pelagian reaction of the Reformers against the idea of a meritorious sacrifice, which is both present and attainable, was right and necessary, and it sums up their opposition to a theology of works and merit. Yet, it may well be asked if out of a *reaction*, which was justified in its beginnings, there has not arisen a theological *position* which involves an unconscious acceptance of the very error which the Reformers were concerned to condemn. The serious error of *popular* Catholic theology in the sixteenth century was to distinguish and to separate our present acts of sacrifice from the one and only true sacrifice of Christ, accomplished once for all on the cross; every mass, every deed became a semi-independent sacrifice, which admittedly derived its value and meaning from that of Christ, but was effective of itself, in so far as it was distinct from that of Christ which was indefinitely repeated. In reaction to this we have rejected all idea of a liturgical sacrifice. The sacrifice of Jesus alone has meaning and value; we have only to preach it and this is the whole of our liturgy.

Nevertheless we continue to live, act and obey within the extension of the life, work and obedience of Christ. Yet the absence of a liturgical way of life compels us to realize the sacrificial work required of us by Christ outside our acts of worship (Rom. 12: 1 f.). This is how the spiritual life, fostered in Protestantism, is directed towards an activity which easily becomes activism and towards a morality which quickly becomes moralism. Both action and moral conduct, instead of being simple signs of gratitude, witness and sanctification, become works, quite unconsciously regarded as meritorious. Popular Catholicism separated the liturgical sacrifice from the unique sacrifice of Christ and turned it into a good work—this is the error of liturgical pietism and formalism; Protestantism, on the other hand, after a healthy reaction against this error, has allowed the separation of action and moral conduct from life in Christ, which is signified and nourished by the liturgy, and has fallen into the error of activism and moralism, another form of Pelagianism.

The Eucharist can restore the sense of unity between the sacrifice of Christ and ours, the unity of faith and works, of the spiritual life and the moral life. Indeed, in the Eucharist, which is the work of God and the Church, as well as the work of the people of God in praise and prayer, the Christian rediscovers the meaning of his life, which is none other than the life of Christ in him (Gal. 2: 20).

Every Eucharist is an act of communion with the intention and with the redemptive work of Christ. It is an active communion with Christ crucified and risen, in the fervour and joy of the Holy Spirit. The Eucharist is the prayer of the Son to the Father, in His Body the Church, through the Holy Spirit. It is a reproduction, within the Church, of the ineffable eternal relations between the Three Persons. It enables the Church to enter into the mystery of the Trinity.

THE HEAVENLY INTERCESSION

Whenever the Church celebrates the Eucharist it enters into close relation with its Lord and gives a constantly renewed form to His unique and eternal intercession.

The Eucharist is one of the essential forms of the life of Christ, as Priest and Intercessor, within the Church. The Church has to receive into its liturgy the unique and eternal intercession of Christ, crucified and risen. The attitude of prayer in the early Church, revealed by the "Orantes" in the Roman catacombs with their arms raised to the skies, expresses exactly what the Church desires in its eucharistic prayer, viz. to offer its life to the Holy Spirit that He may manifest the unique priestly intercession of Jesus, the eternal Priest after the order of Melchizedek. This intercession has been lived in history once for all on the cross, but it continues to live eternally in heaven and sacramentally in Christ's Body the Church. The Church manifests and applies the redemptive intercession of the Son of God through the Eucharist, which makes visible and present His passion and resurrection.

The Church, in the position of an "orans", its arms opened crosswise and lifted on high, reproduces the action of Christ the only Priest and receives into itself His unique intercession. It offers itself to the action of the Holy Spirit, who Himself intercedes for it with groanings that cannot be uttered.

In a very fine passage Luther has shown how the heavenly intercession of Christ and the Church's offering are closely united in the Eucharist:

"We do not offer Christ, it is Christ who offers us (to God). In this way it is permissible and even useful to call the ceremony a sacrifice, not in itself, but because we offer ourselves thereby as a sacrifice with Christ. An alternative way of expressing this is to say that we rest ourselves upon Christ with a firm faith in His covenant, and we only present ourselves before God with our prayer, our praise and our sacrifice in the name of Christ and through His mediation . . . without doubting that He is our priest in heaven before the face of God . . . Christ welcomes us; He presents us (to God), our prayer and our praise; He also offers Himself in heaven for us . . . He offers Himself for us in heaven and offers us with Himself."[1]

In order to reserve to Christ the whole initiative in the eucharistic sacrifice, Luther avoids the formula, which du Moulin was prepared

[1] Sermon on the Mass, 1520, Weimar-Ausgabe, VI, p. 369.

to use, "to offer Christ". But this is not the important point. For Luther, the eucharistic sacrifice consists in the union of the Church's offering with the offering of Christ in His heavenly intercession.

John Wesley's understanding of the Eucharist was very much bound up with its connexion with the heavenly intercession of Christ,[1] and his eucharistic hymns are most striking. The doctrine they express is to the effect that the Lord, sacrificed once upon the cross, has entered the heavenly sanctuary and there pleads for us by means of His sacrifice; the Church is joined to this action by the Eucharist.[2] This sacrificial understanding of the Eucharist is expressed, for example, in the following:

> Turn from me Thy glorious eyes
> To that bloody Sacrifice . . .
> To the tokens of His death
> Here exhibited beneath.[3]

The hymn is indeed a prayer, inviting the Lord to look upon the sacrifice of the cross and the sacrifice of the Eucharist, which is the sign of it presented and exhibited. In another hymn we find:

> Him in a memorial show,
> Offer up the Lamb to God.[4]

This vision of the Lamb presented to God as a memorial is also found in a hymn to Christ:

> Thou stand'st the ever-slaughter'd Lamb,
> Thy priesthood still remains the same.[5]

The eucharistic doctrine of John Wesley is then a fundamentally biblical and traditional expression of the idea of the memorial and of the connexion between the Eucharist and the heavenly intercession of Christ. It is interesting to discover this conception as forming part of the thought of the father of Methodism.

The Presbyterian liturgy in the *Book of Common Order of the Church*

[1] J. E. Rattenbury, *The Eucharistic Hymns of John and Charles Wesley*, 1948; J. C. Bowmer, *The Lord's Supper in Early Methodism*, 1951.

[2] W. M. F. Scott, "The Eucharist and the Heavenly Ministry of our Lord", *Theology*, LVI, 1953, pp. 42–50.

[3] Rattenbury, *op. cit.*, pp. 232 f.

[4] *Ibid.*, p. 232.

[5] *Ibid.*, p. 196.

of Scotland[1] has a very felicitous formula to express this union with the heavenly intercession of Christ:

> We bless Thee for His holy incarnation, for His perfect life on earth, for His precious sufferings and death upon the Cross, for His glorious resurrection and ascension, for His continual intercession and rule at Thy right hand, for the promise of His coming again, and for His gift of the Holy Spirit. Wherefore, having in remembrance the work and passion of our Saviour Christ, and pleading His eternal sacrifice, we Thy servants do set forth this memorial, which He hath commanded us to make.

This setting forth of the memorial in communion with the heavenly intercession of Christ, which is founded upon His sacrifice on the cross, is a very exact expression of the eucharistic sacrifice. And moreover this memorial is later explained to be a sacrifice of thanksgiving and an intercession, closely linked with the act of communion:

> And here we offer and present unto Thee ourselves, our souls and bodies, to be a reasonable, holy, and living sacrifice; and we beseech Thee mercifully to accept this our sacrifice of praise and thanksgiving, as, in fellowship with all the faithful in heaven and on earth, we pray Thee to fulfil in us, and in all men, the purpose of Thy redeeming love.[2]

The eucharistic sacrifice pleads for the application of salvation to all men, since the accomplishing of salvation in the faithful until the return of Christ and the gift of redemption to men who do not yet know it, and all other blessings sought, are relative to this universal salvation, within the perspective of the Kingdom which is to come.

Indeed, if Christ has accomplished everything for the salvation of all men, and if redemption and reconciliation have been achieved on the cross, it remains for the Church, as the Body of Christ, to be the instrument by which all these gifts of salvation may be applied to each and every one in view of the return of the Lord and the manifestation of the Kingdom. Through the Eucharist, as a sacrifice of intercession, the Church is united to the heavenly intercession of Christ, and this is based upon His sacrifice on the cross; and the Church prays to the Father on behalf of all men, for the remission of their sins, for their salvation and happiness, and pleads for the glorious manifestation of the Kingdom:

> Come grace, and let this world pass away . . .
> *Marana tha*, Lord, come.[3]

---

[1] First published 1940, most recent reprint 1957, p. 119.
[2] *Ibid.*, p. 120.
[3] *Didache* 10: 6.

THE CHURCH'S OFFERING

In communion with the heavenly intercession of Christ and with His sacrifice on the cross, and by presenting the memorial of that sacrifice to the Father as an act of praise and supplication, the Church offers herself, each believer offers himself, in adoration and consecration. As Luther wrote: "We present ourselves before God only with our prayer, our praise and our sacrifice in the name of Christ and through His mediation." And Calvin: Jesus Christ in the heavenly sanctuary "is the altar on which we lay our gifts, that whatever we attempt, we may attempt in Him".

Of itself the Church can neither offer nor present anything to God except its misery, but in Christ it can offer a true sacrifice of thanksgiving and intercession, because it can present to the Father the sacrifice of the cross by being united to the heavenly intercession of the Son; it presents the Body of Christ and presents itself as the Body of Christ. This is its true act of praise, its effective prayer, its sacrifice "blessed, approved, ratified, reasonable, acceptable"[1] to God, because it is the very sacrifice of Christ presented by Himself in heaven.

The Church's offertory, when it brings its material and spiritual goods to the altar, is a kind of movement, involving an offering, which precipitates a crisis. When the Church has gathered everything together to offer it to God, it realizes its poverty; there is nothing left for it to do but to remit this misery into the hands of Christ who, gathering it up into His own sacrifice presented in intercession, makes it into a true act of praise, an effective prayer, a sacrifice which is acceptable "by him, and with him, and in him".[2]

This "crisis" at the offertory, which is gathered up by Christ into His sacrifice and intercession, is sometimes indicated by a prayer between the offertory and the eucharistic prayer in which the memorial of Christ's sacrifice will be presented to the Father in praise and supplication. Thus, to take one example from the *secreta* of the Roman rite, that of the second Sunday in Advent:

Permit Thyself to be touched, O Lord, by the prayers and offerings which we present to Thee in our misery, and since we have no merit to put forward to commend us to Thee, come to our aid with Thy riches, through Jesus Christ, Thy Son, our Lord.

[1] Roman rite.
[2] As in the Roman rite.

IV

THE REAL PRESENCE

IT HAS BEEN my concern in this study to examine the sacrificial character of the Eucharist in the light of the biblical memorial; it has not been my concern to consider the problem of Christ's real presence in the sacrament, although this is a subject which has been the centre of much attention. There is no lack of books relating to it and, amongst the most recent, mention may be made of F. J. Leenhardt's *This is My Body*,[1] a work of major importance and most ecumenical in its approach. I do not find myself in any disagreement with what the author has to say about the real presence,[2] nor do I wish merely to repeat what others have already written so excellently about the subject. But it is my concern to draw certain conclusions from my examination of the memorial and the eucharistic sacrifice in order to show that this study issues quite naturally in an affirmation of the real presence of Christ in the mystery of the Eucharist. When the Church performs, in the Eucharist, the unique memorial of the Lord, described above, then Christ is really there present. The Lord's memorial, which is the sacrament of the cross and of the heavenly intercession of Christ, has no meaning unless the Lord Himself is sacramentally present in the Eucharist; otherwise the memorial is no more than a symbolic performance, which may be moving but would have no ontological reality. It is because of the real presence of Christ in the Eucharist that there can be a true memorial of the Lord and a true eucharistic sacrifice in the biblical sense. All that I have said has no reality or meaning unless Christ Himself, really and personally present, acts in the Eucharist as Priest, offering and means of sustenance.

The real and personal presence of Christ in the bread and the wine, which are His body and blood, is a mystery which the Church can never fathom or explain. It can only be presented as an indisputable

---

[1] This is the second part of O. Cullmann and F. J. Leenhardt, *Essays on the Lord's Supper* (Ecumenical Studies in Worship 1), 1958.

[2] I have certain reservations about Ch. IV, "The Lord's Supper as a Sacrifice". The extent to which I differ from Leenhardt will be quite obvious.

fact, and belief in the real presence must be defended against any explanation which either underestimates or overestimates it and against both spiritualization and magic. In a remarkable passage Irenaeus expresses himself about the mystery of the real presence thus: "For as the bread, which is produced from the earth, when it receives the invocation of God, is no longer common bread but the Eucharist, consisting of two realities, earthly and heavenly; so also our bodies, when they receive the Eucharist, are no longer corruptible, having the hope of the resurrection to eternity."[1] And elsewhere: "when, therefore, the mingled cup and the manufactured bread receive the Word of God, and the Eucharist of the blood and body of Christ is made, from which things the substance of our flesh is increased and supported, how can they affirm that the flesh is incapable of receiving the gift of God, which is life eternal, which flesh is nourished from the body and blood of the Lord, and is a member of Him? . . . that flesh which is nourished by the cup which is His blood, and receives increase from the bread which is His body. And just as a cutting from the vine planted in the ground fructifies in its season, or as a corn of wheat falling into the earth and becoming decomposed rises with manifold increase by the Spirit of God, who contains all things, and then, through the wisdom of God, serves for the use of men, and having received the Word of God, becomes the Eucharist, which is the body and blood of Christ; so also our bodies, being nourished by it and deposited in the earth and suffering decomposition there, shall rise at the appointed time."[2]

Would to God that we had remained content with these simple statements concerning the real presence which safeguard its mystery, and had not weighed ourselves down with pseudo-explanations of that which can only be shown forth and accepted in faith! Nevertheless one must not condemn those theologians who throughout the centuries have been concerned to preserve belief in the real presence against dangerous deviations. Indeed the doctrine of transubstantiation was intended to safeguard the truth of the real presence. It was not a rational explanation of the mystery, but a categorical affirmation of the reality of Christ's presence. Unfortunately the terminology employed, developed to safeguard and present the real presence, not to explain it or make it intelligible, became confusing and was not correctly understood in the sixteenth century either by many of the

---

[1] *Adv. Haer.*, IV, 18: 5.
[2] *Ibid.*, V, 2: 3.

Catholic theologians who continued to use it or by Protestants who rejected it.

The Council of Trent, in its thirteenth session on October 11, 1551, first of all affirmed the real presence[1] and then considered the doctrine of transubstantiation.[2] The Council spoke of the real presence as a "conversion" (*conversio*) of the bread and the wine into the body and blood of Christ, "which conversion is conveniently and rightly termed (*appellata*) transubstantiation by the holy Catholic Church". The Council considered "that the Catholic Church calls this conversion, in the most appropriate manner (*aptissime*), transubstantiation". Thus transubstantiation is above all a term, a name, which denotes the reality of Christ's presence, "truly, really and substantially" present in the Eucharist.

Luther also affirmed with equal force that the bread and the wine are the body and blood of Christ, but he rejected transubstantiation in the belief that it was intended to be an explanation: "The sacrament of the altar is the true body and the true blood of our Lord Jesus Christ, under the bread and the wine in order that we Christians may eat and drink, and this was instituted by Christ Himself."[3] In the *Schmalkaldic Articles* of 1537, Luther wrote: "We are not concerned with the sophistic subtlety of transubstantiation . . . For that which is most in accordance with the Scriptures is that the bread is there and remains there, and St. Paul himself calls it: The bread which we break, and, So let him eat of the bread (1 Cor. 10: 16; 11: 28)".[4] Luther's pre-occupation with the Bible led him to affirm both the real presence of Christ's body and blood, in and under the bread and wine, and the natural and chemical persistence of the bread and the wine. Luther indeed wished to maintain the integrity of the mystery and at the same time to employ nothing but the terminology of the New Testament: "This is my *body* . . . The *bread* which we break."

THE CALVINISTIC DOCTRINE OF THE REAL PRESENCE

Calvin affirmed the real presence in a totally different manner: "We have then to confess that if the representation which God grants in the Supper is veracious, the internal substance of the sacrament is joined

[1] C. I, can. 1.
[2] C. IV, can. 2.
[3] *The Little Catechism*, VI; the *Great Catechism* reads, "in and under the bread and the wine".
[4] Part III, art. VI.

with the visible signs; and as the bread is distributed by hand, so the body of Christ is communicated to us, so that we are made partakers of it."[1] Substance, for Calvin, did not denote a kind of invisible material substratum nor the natural and carnal body which was the matter of the physical body of Christ; for him the term substance denoted the fundamental reality of a being or thing.[2] Calvin's doctrine of the Eucharist is that of an effective sign. His terms must be understood if we are to appreciate both the value and the difficulties of his teaching. First of all it must be said that Calvin wished to sustain an ecumenical position between Zwingli and Luther. The next passage to be quoted sheds light on the idea of a sign applied to the Eucharist and it will be seen that Calvin's great concern was to preserve the twofold character of the Eucharist, earthly and heavenly, in the terms of Irenaeus:

"Our Lord, wishing at his Baptism to give visible appearance to his Spirit, represented it under the form of a dove. John the Baptist, relating this story, says that he saw the Holy Spirit descending. If we inquire more closely, we find that he saw only the dove, for the Holy Spirit is essentially invisible. Yet knowing that this vision is not an empty figure, but a certain sign of the presence of the Holy Spirit, he does not hesitate to say that he saw it, because it was represented to him according to his capacity. It is like this with the communion which we have with the body and blood of our Lord. It is a spiritual mystery, which cannot be seen by the eye, nor comprehended by the human understanding. It is therefore symbolized by visible signs, as our infirmity requires, but in such a way that it is not a bare figure, but joined to its reality and substance. It is therefore with good reason that the bread is called body, since not only does it represent it to us, but also presents it to us."[3]

Not only does the sign represent communion with the body and blood of Christ, not only does this, represented, willed by God and accompanied by His promises, assure the Christian in his faith, but also, because of the profound meaning which the sign has for Calvin, it "presents" the reality which it signifies.

Before continuing, certain observations must be made to oppose the belief that the virtue and efficacy of the sacrament are related merely to the fact that it belongs to the category of signs and symbols. While

[1] *Short Treatise on the Lord's Supper,* ed. Reid, *op. cit.,* p. 148.

[2] For an analysis of Calvin's understanding of substance see H. Gollwitzer, *Coena Domini,* 1937, pp. 120 ff.

[3] Reid, *op. cit.,* p. 147.

it is true to say with Thomas Aquinas that *sacramentum ponitur in genere signi*,[1] it is also necessary to define its character to distinguish it from other revealed or natural signs and symbols, lest one fall into the error of natural theology, which seeks to lay hold upon the supernatural by means of natural realities, to grasp the superior by the inferior, by following the path of analogy.

Although the symbol, or sign, conducts the spirit in a mysterious way to the truth signified, the relation it creates between the object signified and the thinking being is subjective and belongs to the sphere of intellect or psychology. The symbol is a powerful means of apprehension or feeling. The sacrament, in so far as it is a symbol or sign, is all that but it is also more because of the will of Him who instituted it. It not only leads the spirit, in an infallible and mysterious manner, to the truth signified, it also assures the presence and effect of the reality symbolized. The sacrament, in so far as it is a revealed sign, allows faith to apprehend fully the truth of the body and blood of Christ as sustenance; in so far as it is a sacrament or effective sign, it truly conveys that which it symbolizes; it conveys the body and blood of Christ as spiritual sustenance.

This understanding of the sign, which is also that of the Fathers, led Calvin to the idea of the real presence: the Eucharist is a sign which gives assurance, and because it is a sign and gives assurance, that which is signified and assured must be really present, otherwise the sign would be empty and the assurance vain.

The Eucharist is an effective sign because its substance is Christ Himself. "The matter and substance of the sacrament is the Lord Jesus Christ, and the efficacy of them is the gifts and blessings which we have by means of him."[2] Calvin and, following him, Reformed doctrine as a whole go very far in their affirmation of the real presence. "Christ with all His riches is presented in it (the Eucharist) no less than if He were set before our eyes and were touched by our hands."[3] In the *Short Treatise on the Lord's Supper*, Reformed teaching is summed up in these words: "We all confess, then, with one mouth that, in receiving the sacrament in faith, according to the ordinance of the Lord, we are truly made partakers of the real substance of the body and blood of Jesus Christ."[4]

[1] *Summa*, IIIa Pars, q. 60, a. 1.
[2] Reid, *op. cit.*, p. 146.
[3] *Instruction*, 1537, art. "Of the Lord's Supper".
[4] Reid, *op. cit.*, p. 166.

Had Calvin remained content with a simple affirmation of the real presence, an understanding with the Lutherans might have been possible; but Zwingli disturbed him with his rationalist questions. The mystical imprecision of Luther did not satisfy him and he said of him that "he added some similes which were a little hard and rude . . . For it is difficult to give an explanation of so high a matter, without using some impropriety of speech."[1]

Finally we come to Calvin's doctrine of the role of the Holy Spirit in the Eucharist.[2]

Calvin's thought may be briefly summed up like this: Christ, with His glorified body, has ascended into heaven, and from thence He will come to judge the quick and the dead at the end of the ages. It would involve a misconception of the human body, even a glorified one, or it would involve making this body a phantom, like the Gnostics and the Docetists who denied the incarnation, if it were to be supposed that the body could come to be united locally with the eucharistic elements. It is the Holy Spirit who establishes this "connexion" between the body and blood of Christ and the sacramental signs; the Holy Spirit is there as "a kind of channel by which everything that Christ has and is is derived to us",[3] and Calvin goes on to compare Christ with the sun and the Holy Spirit with the rays which come to bring its warmth to the earth.

Calvin and indeed Reformed teaching as a whole have never been entirely at ease with this explanation of the mystery. Calvin showed some hesitancy in his *Short Treatise on the Lord's Supper* in which he asserted: "It is not only a matter of being partakers of his Spirit; it is necessary also to partake of his humanity, in which he rendered complete obedience to God his Father, to satisfy our debts."[4]

Later in the same work, in order to refute the idea of a local presence, he declared:

"Now to maintain this (the localized presence), it is necessary to confess either that the body of Christ is without limit, or that it can be in different places. In saying so, we come at last to the point where it appears nothing but a phantom. Hence to wish to establish such a presence that the body of Christ is enclosed within the signs, or is

---

[1] *Ibid.*, p. 164.
[2] He derived his conception from a sermon attributed to John Chrysostom by Erasmus and printed in the edition of his works published at Basel in 1530.
[3] *Inst.*, IV. xvii. 12.
[4] Reid, *op. cit.*, p. 146.

joined locally to it, is not only a dream but a damnable error, contradicting the glory of Christ, and destructive of what we ought to hold concerning his human nature. For Scripture teaches us everywhere, that as our Lord Jesus Christ on earth took our humanity, so he has exalted it into heaven, withdrawing it from its mortal condition, but not changing its nature. So we have two things to consider when we speak of our Lord's humanity. We may not destroy the reality of his nature, nor derogate at all from its glorious estate. To observe this rightly, we have always to raise our thoughts on high, to seek our Redeemer. For if we wish to abase him under the corruptible elements of this world, besides subverting what Scripture declares concerning his human nature, we annihilate the glory of his ascension."[1] Finally, at the end of the treatise, he gives a summary of his teaching: "How this is done (our participation in the substance of Christ) some may deduce better and explain more clearly than others. But be this as it may, on the one hand we must, to shut out all carnal fancies, raise our hearts on high to heaven, not thinking that our Lord Jesus Christ is so abased as to be enclosed under any corruptible elements. On the other hand, not to diminish the efficacy of this sacred mystery, we must hold that it is accomplished by the secret and miraculous virtue of God, and that the Spirit of God is the bond of participation, for which reason it is called spiritual."[2]

Statements of Reformed doctrine which refer to spiritual participation in the body and blood of Christ should not be interpreted in terms of a liberal spiritualization which sees communion as an act of man's comprehending the symbol; they mean that the body and blood of Christ are really communicated with the signs by the "channel" of the Holy Spirit.

In his exposition of the real presence, Calvin seems to have had a too carnal conception of the body of Christ. Despite his great emphasis on the humanity of Jesus, Calvin did not sufficiently appreciate the difference of condition between Christ living and suffering, from the Annunciation to Calvary, and Christ risen and glorified, from Easter to the Ascension and in eternity. He too easily identified the condition of Him who was crucified and of Him who was glorified. It is possible that Calvin tended to separate the divine and human natures in Christ and did not sufficiently appreciate their unity, in the sense of the

[1] Reid, *op. cit.*, pp. 158 f.
[2] *Ibid.*, p. 166.

prologue to John: "The Word became flesh" (1: 14). There would seem to be a kind of alternation of the divine and human in Calvin's Christology. While firmly holding to the humanity of Christ—and this comes out in all his preaching, which presents Christ as truly man like us—Calvin was not always free from a certain Docetism, although this statement may seem inconsistent. This is the basis of his rejection of any representation of Christ by means of an image and his refusal to allow a crucifix. There is a radiance of Christ's divinity which it would be impious to try to represent or impious to refuse to represent by the pretence of depicting His humanity alone. In the first case one would come under the condemnation of the second commandment; in the second one would be injuring the mystery of the incarnation and the union of the two distinct natures. Calvin certainly confessed the reality of the incarnation, but he did not appreciate it in all its depth; he did not sufficiently realize that the incarnation is a humiliation (Phil. 2: 7). It often seems that to him Christ came *with the flesh* and did not really *become flesh*. Indeed the distinction of the two natures is in general over-emphasized in Calvinism and the unity of Christ is reduced to one of juxtaposition.

This explains, on the one hand, the character of Jesus which is seen to be both human and radiant with divinity, even in His passion on the cross, which makes strict Calvinists reject any representation of the Son of man, and, on the other hand, the nature of the risen humanity of Christ, sitting at His Father's right hand, which is both glorious and limited.

This too emphatic distinction between the two natures in Christ explains the tendency of Calvinism to fail to appreciate the difference between Christ up to the crucifixion and Christ after the resurrection. It is important to notice this in connexion with the Reformed doctrine of the sacrament, because it creates one of its greatest difficulties. New Testament Christology, and especially that formulated in the fourth Gospel, helps to expose this difficulty and to overcome it, correcting the too-restrained conception that Calvin, in his concern to counteract the dogmatic excesses of Luther, had of the body of Christ.

"*Haec est perpetua corporis veritas, ut loco contineatur, ut suis dimensionibus constet*", wrote Calvin in 1536. One may well ask if this restrained definition of the body can be applied to the conception of the "glorious body" developed by St. Paul in 1 Cor. 15 and St. John's conception of Christ's body after the resurrection.

It is very noticeable how St. John, the witness of the incarnation,

which he made the centre of the Christian faith, takes pains to emphasize the mysterious nature of Christ's body after the resurrection.
John wrote his Gospel in the light of the phrase in his preface: "The
Word became flesh." In his first Epistle he states that "every spirit
which confesseth that Jesus Christ is come in the flesh is of God" (4: 2).
Jesus Christ then, true Son of God, true God, has become man, He has
become flesh, "*he emptied himself*, taking the form of a servant, being
made in the likeness of men" (Phil. 2: 7). "He hath no form nor
comeliness; and when we see him, there is no beauty that we should
desire him" (Is. 53: 2); there was indeed no "physical" and natural
radiation in the person of Christ. He was truly like us, and the whole
power of the Holy Spirit was necessary to bring faith to life in the
disciples' hearts that they might recognize God in this humble itinerant
preacher. There is no point in advancing the objection that He performed miracles and that they revealed His divinity and enclosed it in
a kind of halo. The miracle is for the man of faith; it is an act of
condescension to human weakness, by means of which God strengthens
the imperfect faith of His people. And miracles were all the more
necessary during Jesus' earthly life because His human presence was a
"scandal" for faith. How could one believe that this poor man was
God Himself? Miracles add nothing to him who has no faith in the
Holy Spirit. "If they hear not Moses and the prophets, neither will
they be persuaded, if one rise from the dead" (Lk. 16: 31). Miracles
indeed are always capable of a physical or psychological explanation.
Renan showed this quite clearly. A miracle is a miracle only to faith.

Jesus then truly "emptied himself" in His humanity from cradle to
cross. He was like any other man and must be pictured as any other
man. The mystery of the two natures is discernible only by faith.

After His resurrection, the humanity of Jesus was veiled by His
divinity, as previously His humanity had veiled His divinity. He had
to perform miracles of power to strengthen the faith of His disciples
in His divinity, but now He performs miracles of humility to prove
to them that He is always near them, as man, unto the end of the
world. Once He calmed the storm and walked on the waves, now He
eats with His own, as man, and allows Himself to be touched by
Thomas (Lk. 24: 41 f.; Jn. 20: 27).

The mystery of the glorified body of Christ is strongly emphasized
by the accounts of the resurrection appearances, particularly in Luke
and John. He told Mary Magdalene not to touch Him, as if it were
abnormal that, in His glorified state, He should be visible to His

followers, while His condition required His presence with the Father. It was to justify the faith of His followers that He was prepared to show Himself for forty days (Jn. 20: 17). Elsewhere, He invited the astonished and doubting disciples to touch Him, a condescension to the weakness of their faith (Lk. 24: 39). He entered the house where the disciples were "when the doors were shut" (20: 19, 26), thus revealing the new and glorious nature of His body. Yet He ate with the apostles, taking a piece of grilled fish and showing thereby the humanity of His person.

All these references bear witness to the new character of the person of the Risen Christ. Although He continues to be human, although He continues to be the Word incarnate, He now has a new body, assumed into the glory of His Godhead. This body cannot be defined within the limits that apply to an ordinary human body; it cannot be restricted by place or size, as Calvin expressed it. This body belongs to the mystery, and the presence of Christ's body at the Eucharist should be understood in accordance with the mystery of the Lord's resurrection appearances to His disciples, from Easter to the Ascension.

Because of his restricted idea of the body of Christ, Calvin localized it in heaven, in an entirely anthropomorphic manner, and invited us to "raise our hearts on high to heaven" to find our Lord there "who is not so abased as to be enclosed under any corruptible elements".

This is obviously a reaction against the peculiar Lutheran idea of the ubiquity of Christ's body. The Lutherans maintained that the glorified body of Christ, because of its assumption into the Godhead, could derive benefit from the advantages of the Godhead, viz. amongst other things, the possibility of being everywhere at once or ubiquity. This was an awkward attempt to explain the mysterious nature of the risen and glorified body and its real presence at the Eucharist.

Calvin's conception of the body of Christ then seems somewhat deficient, especially as it is expressed in his theology of the sacrament and of the real presence; but there is a second difficulty: his doctrine of the Holy Spirit. Calvin, together with all orthodox Reformed theologians, believed in the Trinity and affirmed the divine personality of the Spirit. But actually Calvin minimized the personal character of the Spirit by his application of the doctrine to his sacramental theology. According to the role ascribed to Him at the Eucharist, the Holy Spirit is the Spirit of Christ, "a kind of channel by which everything that Christ has, and is, is derived to us". Later Christ is compared with the sun and the Spirit with its rays which convey its substance to the earth; again it is a question of the "light and radiance" of the Spirit of

Christ. All these expressions indicate a certain irresolution in Calvin's doctrine of the Spirit. The Spirit is no longer so much the third Person of the Trinity as an instrument of the Son, and so the Spirit of the Son. We have passed quietly from a personal conception to an instrumental one. The Spirit, when His activity is expressed in terms of eucharistic doctrine, becomes "the bond of that connexion" between the person of Christ, localized "in heaven", and the faith of the communicant, by means of the elements. The Spirit is no more than a unifying power reducing the distance between Christ and the believer.

When Calvin's difficulty in relation to Luther has been appreciated, as well as his concern to preserve the full humanity of the glorified Christ, it must still be acknowledged that the Reformer believed firmly in the real presence of the body and blood of Christ;[1] so he wrote to Bullinger on December 27, 1562: "Although the flesh of Christ is in heaven, we nevertheless feed truly upon it on earth, because Christ by the unfathomable and omnipresent power of His Spirit makes Himself so much ours that He dwells in us without change of place . . . I see no absurdity in saying that we really receive the flesh and blood of Christ and that He is thus substantially our food, provided that it be agreed that Christ descends to us not merely by the exterior symbols but also by the secret operation of His Spirit, that we may ascend to Him by faith."[2]

Whatever the dogmatic or exegetical difficulties of Calvin's doctrine, it must be recognized that His devotion demanded the most positive affirmations concerning the real presence, while at the same time these doctrinal preoccupations did not allow him to express himself with complete clarity. Moreover Calvin desired to respect the mystery of

[1] F. Wendel, *Calvin, sources et évolution de sa pensée religieuse*, 1950, pp. 251–71; A. Graf, "La doctrine calvinienne de la sainte cène", *Revue de théologie et de philosophie*, LXXXIII, 1932, pp. 135–50. See also: W. Niesel, *Calvins Lehre vom Abendmahl*, 1935; E. Bizer, *Studien zur Geschichte des Abendmahlstreites im 16. Jahrhundert*, 1940; J. Cadier, *La doctrine calviniste de la sainte cène*, 1951.

[2] See Calvin's *Commentary* on I Cor. 11:24: "My conclusion is that the body of Christ is really, to use the usual word, i.e. truly given to us in the Supper, so that it may be health-giving food for our souls. I am adopting the usual terms, but I mean that our souls are fed by the substance of His body, so that we are truly made one with Him; or, what amounts to the same thing, that a life-giving power from the flesh of Christ is poured into us through the medium of the Spirit, even although it is at a great distance from us, and is not mixed with us" (*The First Epistle of Paul the Apostle to the Corinthians*, trans. J. W. Fraser, 1960, p. 246).

the Eucharist and of the real presence, and he asserted: "As for myself, I am overcome with astonishment at the incomprehensible excellence of this secret, and I am not ashamed to confess my ignorance as, with St. Paul, I marvel at it. For is it not better to act in this way than to diminish, through my fleshly understanding, what St. Paul declares to be a great mystery? And reason itself teaches us to act in this way, for everything that is supernatural surpasses our capacity to understand. Wherefore let us affirm that we feel Christ living within us, and let us not assert that the means of this communion have been made known to us."[1]

Pierre Martyr Vermigli, the friend of Theodore of Beza, declared at the Colloquy of Poissy in 1561: "The substance of His flesh and blood are truly promised, offered and given to us . . . The Holy Spirit, by His secret and ineffable operation, effects in us on earth this communion and participation in the body that dwells in heaven and not elsewhere, thus accommodating His majesty to our capacity, and as if He were visibly uniting heaven and earth by His power to erect His royal throne in the midst of the Eucharist and to give pasture to our souls."[2]

The Reformed Church has always been concerned to preserve belief in the real presence; thus, in 1931, the Synod of the Reformed Churches of France declared:

"As concerning the mode of the Lord's presence in the sacrament, believers can have different views, but they cannot differ on the fact of the presence itself; it is a real presence according to the Spirit and is inseparable from the elements of the Eucharist in the very act of celebration."

The Eastern Orthodox, more than Western Christians, have had this respect for the mystery of the real presence without attempting to overdefine its mode. Before the sixteenth century, the majority of Orthodox theologians wisely refused to advance beyond a simple belief in the real presence and the idea of a change of the bread and wine into the body and blood of Christ, without defining this change in philosophical terms. Some, who had read St. Thomas, introduced the idea of transubstantiation, but without explanation or illustrations to make it easier to comprehend. After the sixteenth century three tendencies may be noted: (i) that which retains the idea of transubstanti-

---

[1] Calvin's *Commentary* on Eph. 5: 32; he applies the "great mystery" to the Eucharist and criticizes those who wish to know the mode of the real presence before believing in it.

[2] Quoted by J. Cadier, *op. cit.*, p. 113.

ation; (ii) that which accepts the doctrine of Trent, without explaining transubstantiation; (iii) that which is content to affirm the reality of the presence, while rejecting even the idea of the permanence of the accidents.

It is to be noted that all these tendencies, eastern or western, have a close connexion with the different Christological positions adopted and the different conceptions of the relation between the two natures. Those who have a tendency to separate the humanity and divinity (a Nestorian attitude) also have a tendency to separate the bread from the body and the wine from the blood of Christ and find it difficult to express the connexion between the eucharistic elements and the person of Christ. In the fourteenth century, Timothy II, a Nestorian patriarch, expressed himself thus: "This bread and this wine, which are not by nature either body or blood, are called by the grace of the Holy Spirit which is poured upon us body and blood of Christ . . . Since we say that the bread and the wine are body and blood by grace, it cannot be supposed that they are God by nature."[1] Those who have a tendency to confuse the humanity and divinity (a Monophysite attitude)[2] also have a tendency to confuse the bread and the body and the wine and the blood, by refusing to maintain even the Catholic distinction between the substance which changes and the accidents which persist. In this connexion, as with Christology, the teaching of Chalcedon should be respected. Although the substance of the Eucharist, its basic reality, is the body and blood of Christ, its chemical nature remains bread and wine, and we cannot define the mode of their relation, which is, however, such (as the Scriptures compel us to acknowledge) that the Eucharist *is* the body and the blood of Christ.

THESES CONCERNING THE REAL PRESENCE

1. The body and blood of Christ, His whole humanity and deity, are truly, really and substantially present in the Eucharist.

---

[1] *De sacramentis*, ed. Assémani, *Bibliotheca orientalis*, III, pp. 294 f.; W. de Vries, *Sakramenten Theologie bei den Nestorianern, Orientalia Christiana analecta*, 133, 1947, pp. 214-20. Nestorians always find it difficult to separate ideas of substance and nature from their concrete manifestations. Nestorians at the present day adhere to the orthodox doctrine; see *D.T.C.*, art. *Eucharistie*, col. 1322 ff.

[2] W. de Vries, *Sakramenten Theologie bei den syrischen Monophysiten, Orientalia Christiana analecta*, 125, 1940; I. H. Dalmais, "Note sur la théologie des Mystères dans les Eglises Syriennes (occidentales et orientales)", *Maison-Dieu*, 19, pp. 60 f.: "There is present . . . the ancient semitic conception of holiness as a quasi-physical fluid which may be communicated by touch."

This real presence of His body and blood is the presence of Christ crucified and glorified, here and now, under concrete signs. The meaning of every corporal presence is to attest concretely the presence of that person that he may enter into a concrete communion. By the real presence of His body and blood, the Church knows that Christ is there concretely in the midst and it receives Him by means of a concrete sign. The substantial presence of Christ does not denote a material presence, in the natural sense, but the presence of the profound reality of the body and blood of Christ crucified and glorified.

2. Christ glorified sits at the right hand of the Father in His humanity and in His deity; how it happens that He is also present corporally in the Eucharist is a mystery and the work of the Holy Spirit which the Church cannot define.

The real presence of Christ is not to be understood as a localization limited to the elements of bread and wine; Christ cannot be shut up within the limits of the created world. But the bread and the wine at the Eucharist do become a privileged place where Christ Himself, in His humanity and deity, may be met and received. Christ glorified, by His power to subject all things, acts through the Holy Spirit and by His Word on the bread and the wine, to make them into a place where the Church may meet Him and receive Him corporally, so that they are the instrument through which the Church can reach Him in the fullness of His humanity and deity.

3. Christ then, through the Holy Spirit and His Word, takes sovereign possession of the elements of bread and wine, draws them to Himself and assumes them into the fullness of His humanity and deity, in such a way that they become truly, really and substantially His body and blood.

The glorified Christ takes the bread and wine as a sign to manifest His corporal presence in the Church. The bread and wine of the Eucharist are no longer ordinary bread and wine. Of course their chemical nature remains that of bread and wine, but behind this faith must recognize the true and new substantial reality of the bread and wine: the body and blood of Christ. The Church does not limit itself to the bare fact of the reality of the bread and wine; it also believes that they are changed, not chemically, in the sense that the glorified Christ takes possession of them to make them a concrete sign of His presence in our midst, to make them His body and blood, a place where He may be found locally, contemplated sensibly and communicated concretely.

4. It is the Holy Spirit, requested of the Father, and the Word of Christ, uttered by the Church, in the course of the memorial performed in the great eucharistic prayer, that make the bread and the wine the body and blood of Christ.

It is not necessary to determine the precise moment at which the mystery is accomplished. It is by means of the whole liturgical action, and especially by the whole eucharistic prayer (from the *Sursum corda* to the *Amen*) that the bread and wine are eucharistized by the Holy Spirit and the Word of Christ, in the memorial presented to the Father. In the unfolding of the liturgical movement a privileged moment at which consecration is effected is not to be selected nor must a tension be created between the words of Christ and the invocation of the Holy Spirit. The normal liturgical order would be for the Holy Spirit to be invoked before the words of institution to signify that He gives them life and actuality, in such a way that they become the Lord's body and blood. A second epiclesis or invocation may have its place after the words of institution and the anamnesis, but in this instance they prepare the congregation to receive the body and blood of Christ. Two such invocations are to be found in the old Alexandrian liturgy of St. Mark.

5. The figure of the bread and the wine is the sign that Christ is our sustenance; this sign of bread and wine is the vehicle of the real presence of the body and blood of Christ in us. This real and corporal presence should be contemplated and received in the liturgical action when Christ acts with and for us and gives Himself to us in communion.

The Eucharist is not a sacred object, but an action and an act of communion. The signs of bread and wine are eucharistized for the sacrifice of thanksgiving and intercession, which are accomplished in the communion. The sick, who desire it, though they are kept at home, are associated with the eucharistic action; communion may be carried to their homes by what is to be regarded as an extension of the celebration.

6. The body and blood of Christ which are objectively present in the Eucharist for communion really come to those who receive them: to those who have a right intention as a means of sanctification, and to those who will not recognize the Body of Christ, through lack of faith, and the Body of the Church, through egotism, as a means of condemnation.

St. Paul expressed the objectivity of the eucharistic presence of Christ when he pointed out the grave consequences of an unbelieving or egotistical act of communion, without discerning the body of

Christ or the body of the Church by faith and love (1 Cor. 11: 27-34). Where there is an unworthy act of communion, he who lacks faith and love meets Christ, really present, but does not receive the fruits of this encounter: on the contrary he is condemned for the absence of faith and love.

7. After the celebration has been completed by the communion of the faithful, including that of the sick in their homes, the real connexion between Christ and the elements left over is a mystery that should be respected.

Since the conclusion of the Eucharist is the communion ("Take, eat . . . Drink ye all of this"), we cannot define the nature of the relationship of Christ and the elements that remain after the completion of communion. There is no need to speculate about the continuance nor about its disappearance. The mystery is to be respected. Because of such an attitude of respect, it is fitting that the eucharistic remains should be consumed after the celebration.[1] Negligence in this matter tends to compromise belief in the real presence, whereas a balanced respect is a sign of true belief in the presence of the body and blood of Christ and a sign that, at least, the material basis of this presence has a right to our respect. Belief in the efficacy of the Word of Christ involves belief that it will not leave unchanged those created things upon which it comes.

8. Communion in the body and blood of Christ is at the same time

[1] Only sufficient wine for the communion should be consecrated; where an insufficient amount has been consecrated, then more wine should be added to the chalice while it still has some eucharistized wine in it, and this will safeguard the centrality of the eucharistic prayer. Such a practice has its basis in tradition. When the congregation was very large, it was impossible to consecrate all the wine necessary on the altar. The celebrant consecrated only his own chalice and, before communion, the deacons consecrated the chalices for the congregation by adding a little of the wine consecrated by the celebrant or a fragment of consecrated bread. The prayer in the Roman rite: *Haec commixtio et consecratio*, was thus understood literally. Besides, *Haec* replaced a primitive *fiat* after the Council of Trent; thus the meaning of the prayer was: "May the mixture and consecration of the body and blood of our Lord take place." The three signs of the cross made with a particle of the host over the chalice recall this primitive form of consecration; the priest drops the particle into the wine and this is an action which no longer has any meaning in terms of consecration. This complex rite has other origins, but here it is sufficient to note the primitive idea of consecration by mixing a fragment of consecrated bread (or a little consecrated wine) with the wine intended for the communion of the faithful. De Jonge, "L'arrière-plan dogmatique de la commixtion", 1953, quoted by T. Maertens, art. cit. p. 352.

a communion of each individual in the Body of Christ, the Church. United in Christ in one offering by the Church, the faithful are joined indissolubly together by communion in the Body of Christ.

If the Church makes the Eucharist, the Eucharist makes the Church. The Eucharist unifies and joins together the members of the Body of Christ; those who have been baptized are joined together in unity and can but seek the deepening, extension and fulfilment of their unity. As the sacrament of unity, the Eucharist is the sacrament of charity which it supports and extends. Hence, in the quest for the unity of the Church, intercommunion should be seen not as an end but as a means of recognizing and living the fact that Christ establishes the unity of His Body in the communion of His eucharistic body. And in the life of a local community, the Eucharist is the place where the Church is built up and deepened in charity. That Church which celebrates the Eucharist frequently beholds Christ, through the Eucharist, developing His charity, His unity, and making His word and His life effective in the world.

CONCLUSION

BY MEANS OF the Eucharist we are able to send up to God our most
pure thanksgiving for all His blessings and our most fervent intercession
for all our needs; by means of the Eucharist the unique sacrifice of
Christ is present in our midst, and so we receive its benefits now on
our own behalf, and for all mankind; by means of the Eucharist we
are united to the heavenly intercession of Christ and associated with
the praise of all the saints; by means of the Eucharist we receive, truly,
really and substantially the body and blood of Christ and so the fullness
of His divine and human person; by the Eucharist we are united to all
the members of the Church and, as in no other way, our charity is
increased ... how much then should we desire to celebrate the Eucharist
and to communicate frequently in the body and blood of Christ! The
Lord Himself "with desire desired" to eat the Passover with His
disciples. How can we not with desire desire to celebrate and eat the
new Passover, wherein He Himself offers our praises and our supplications by presenting His unique sacrifice, and gives us His body and
blood as sustenance unto life eternal!

Christians cannot but fervently desire this celebration and this
wonderful communion, and among them (especially) the clergy, whose
ministry it is to preach the Word and to celebrate the Sacraments.
According to the ancient discipline of the Reformed Churches, the
celebration of the Eucharist is the particular duty of ministers.[1]

---

[1] F. Méjan, *Discipline de l'Eglise réformée de France*, 1947, pp. 274–78. The Synod
of Saint-Maixent, in 1609, declared: ministers should "alone speak at the distribution of the sacred signs, in order that it may be clearly seen that the admini-
stration of the sacrament is an essential part of their authorized ministry" (p. 277).
Although it is to be desired at the present day that confirmed laity, elders and
deacons should be associated with the minister in the celebration of the Eucharist,
the fact must always be safeguarded that the Eucharist, like the preaching of the
Word, belongs to the ministry of Christ in His Church and that this is signified
by ordained ministers. According to Calvin's *Catechism*, 55 (this is the *catechismus
prior* and not the *catechismus posterior* translated by Reid, *op. cit.*, pp. 83–139):

"Q. To whom does it belong either to baptize or to administer the Supper?
A. To those who have the public charge to teach in the Church ...
Q. Can you prove this from Scripture?
A. Yes; for our Lord gave specially to His apostles the charge to baptize and

How many ministers would find their ministry more balanced by frequent celebrations of the Eucharist! Quite often ministers, after several years of service, are faced with a crisis. This crisis may have several causes, in particular the tendency to lose the essential element in the pastoral ministry by a laicizing of the office. The minister, reduced to the status of a specialized layman, may well ask himself whether or not he would be better employed as a doctor, teacher or journalist.[1] There is a further reason for this crisis, and that is the intellectual character of pastoral work. The minister comes to envy a more practical profession, especially when to a certain intellectual dryness there is added the lack of any visible effect of His preaching and teaching. Happily God watches over His ministers and renews them in due season. He restores the desire to preach, to teach and exercise the cure of souls. . . . But does not the Lord also summon His ministers to nourish themselves frequently with His body and blood, to offer Him thanksgiving and to present to Him the eucharistic intercession?

In frequent celebrations, the minister sees his ministry being extended to the dimensions of the mystery of Christ. Questions of immediate results concern him less, because he knows that it is in the Eucharist that Christ builds up His community and deepens it in unity and charity. He knows that therein he presents to God the purest thanksgiving and the most fervent intercession and that he receives, with the congregation, the body and blood of Christ, which are the power of salvation in the world. There can be no question that the ministry of the Catholic priest is stabilized by his daily celebration of mass. I trust that my intentions will not be misunderstood: my appeal for frequent celebrations (at least weekly, and perhaps even daily) is not based on a

preach. And, as for the Supper, He commands us to celebrate it after His example. So He made the office of minister by giving it to others."

[1] It is to be noted to what extent Reformed discipline has been concerned to define the nature of the different ministries in the Church, their relation to the whole and their degree of permanence. In 1559 it was affirmed: "The office of the deacon is not to preach the Word nor to administer the Sacraments, although they may give assistance; and their authorization is not perpetual, although they may not leave their obedience without the approval of the Churches" (Art. 23). Today the function of a deacon may be defined differently (in 1559, "to visit the poor, the prisoners and the sick, and to go into homes for the purposes of catechizing", Art. 22); but within the context of a clear disciplinary system, each ministry, unique and indispensable, should have a clearly recognized place in the Church. It is to be noted that Article 23, quoted above, allows the interpretation that the ministry of the pastor is perpetual.

vague feeling of nostalgia, but upon the experience of the wonderful power of Christ in the Eucharist, whereby pastoral energies are renewed and the gift, received by the laying on of hands at ordination, is stirred up.

The question of numbers should not arise. At a daily celebration, only one or two of the faithful would probably take part to begin with. But the minister knows that he is performing Christ's action on behalf of His Church, and that, by celebrating the Eucharist through his hands, the Lord is building up the Church.

The realization of this hope will be limited by the tradition of a church or parish. Great patience is needed, but a patience which is fervent. The pastor must first be completely convinced himself, and then, little by little, the influence of his love and hopes will bring the Church and his parish to desire, like the Lord, to eat the new Passover, which its pastor is ready to offer regularly.

Then the cross, that is set up in the midst of the community by means of the Eucharist, will bear fruit in unity and charity, in thanksgiving to God. Then too the revelation of the Kingdom in glory will be besought with fervour, and hastened, for the Eucharist is the special prayer for the return of Christ. "Yea, come, Lord Jesus! *Maranatha!*"

This book, in its French edition, appeared in the quater-centenary year of the first Synod of the Reformed Church of France, which took place in 1559.

I have intended it to be a piece of biblical research which is both in accordance with Reformed tradition and ecumenical in approach.

It is to be hoped that the Churches of the Reformation, impelled by a new thirst for truth in love and unity, will advance even more resolutely along the road of ecumenical co-operation and understanding, so that no Christian and no Church may be excluded.

The Eucharist is the sacrament of unity; the more we extend this mystery of Christ in our midst, the more we desire that Eucharist at which, in a rediscovered unity, we shall communicate from the same bread and from the same cup. Then we should be ready for the new Passover of the Kingdom of God.

When the French edition of this work was in the press, Pope John XXIII announced, on January 25, 1959, the summoning of an ecumenical council to consider the question of unity. Christians everywhere cannot but approve of this in hope.

I should like to finish by offering this book to our Roman Catholic brothers also, as a sign of brotherhood in research. And this conclusion has more point in view of our greater hope. May this work initiate a fruitful dialogue on the Eucharist which is the sacrament of unity, and contribute, however little, to the preparation of a council from which we hope much.

The preparation for an ecumenical council and the preparation for Christian unity require from us all the fervent prayer that every prejudice will be cast off, all misunderstandings resolved and all divisions overcome in a generous charity, which is prepared to make true sacrifices. It is in the Eucharist that our prayers for the visible unity of all Christians can be most fervent, in accordance with this fine prayer:

> O Lord Jesus Christ, who didst say to Thine apostles, Peace I leave with you, my peace I give unto you: Regard not our sins, but the faith of Thy Church, and grant it that peace and unity which is agreeable to Thy will; who livest and reignest with the Father and the Holy Spirit, one God, world without end. Amen.

APPENDIX

I AM PROVIDING here the text of a eucharistic liturgy which is in accordance with the most authentic and universal traditions. The first part, the introit liturgy, is given in three forms; the second part is the liturgy of the Word; in the third part, the liturgy of the Sacrament, I have reproduced the text for the anaphora or eucharistic prayer which is in use at Taizé and is inspired by the best traditions and in conformity with modern developments. I am not suggesting that this is the best liturgy possible or that it should be regarded as providing a norm. The Church alone can promulgate a liturgy, and the movement of liturgical renewal has produced many excellent outlines. My sole intention is to give some indication of the effect my researches may possibly have upon liturgical revision and to provide a formula for study.

The scheme for the introit liturgy which I have termed "simple" would be suitable for a daily celebration at which sermon, hymns and creed were omitted. That which I have termed "primitive" is intended for use on solemn festivals, such as Christmas or Easter. That which I have termed "ordinary" would be suitable for other Sundays in the year, with the possible addition of the Commandments before the Confession in Advent and Lent.

INTROIT LITURGY

(Ordinary) Introit (psalm plus antiphon), Confession, *Kyrie*, Absolution, *Gloria*, Collect.

(Primitive) Introit (psalm plus antiphon), Litany, *Kyrie* (as its response), *Gloria*, Collect.

(Simple) Introit (psalm plus antiphon), Collect.

LITURGY OF THE WORD

Old Testament Lesson, Hymn, Epistle, Alleluia, Gospel, Hymn, Sermon, Creed, Intercession (Mementos).

LITURGY OF THE SACRAMENT

Offertory chant (during the collection of the offerings and the bringing of the bread and wine), Offertory prayer, leading into *Eucharistic prayer:*

> *Sursum corda*
> Preface
> *Sanctus*

Invocation of the Holy Spirit

Our Father, God of the powers of heaven, fill our sacrifice of praise with thy glory.

Bless, perfect and accept this offering as the figure of the one and only sacrifice of our Lord.

Send thy Holy Spirit upon us and upon our Eucharist: consecrate this bread to be the body of Christ and this cup to be the blood of Christ; that the Creator Spirit may fulfil the Word of thy beloved Son.

Institution Narrative

Who, in the night in which he was betrayed, took bread, and, when he had given thanks, he brake it and gave it to his disciples, saying: Take, eat, this is my body which is given for you; do this as the memorial of me.

Likewise, after supper, he took the cup, and, when he had given thanks, he gave it to his disciples, saying: Drink ye all of this, this cup is the new covenant in my blood which is shed for you and for many for the remission of sins; as oft as ye drink this cup, do this as the memorial of me.

So, as oft as we eat this bread and drink this cup, we proclaim the Lord's death until he come.

Memorial

Wherefore, O Lord, we make before thee the memorial of the incarnation and of the passion of thy Son, of his resurrection from his sojourn with the dead, of his ascension into glory into the heavens, of his continual intercession on our behalf; we await and pray for his return.

All comes of thee and our only offering is to recall thy marvellous works and gifts.

We also present unto thee, Lord of glory, as our thanksgiving and intercession, the signs of the eternal sacrifice of Christ, unique and perfect, living and holy, the Bread of life which cometh down from heaven and the Cup of the meal in thy Kingdom.

In thy love and mercy, accept our praise and our prayer in Christ, as thou hast accepted the gifts of thy servant Abel the righteous, the sacrifice of our father Abraham and that of Melchizedek, thy high priest.

Invocation

We beseech thee, almighty God, that this prayer may be borne by the hands of thine angel to the altar on high in thy presence; and when, communicating at this table, we receive the Body and Blood of thy Son, may we be filled with the Holy Spirit and endowed with grace and heavenly blessings, through Christ our Saviour.

Conclusion

It is by him, Lord, that thou dost create, sanctify, quicken, bless and give us all thy benefits.

By him, and with him, and in him, be unto thee, O Father almighty, in the unity of the Holy Spirit, all honour and glory, world without end. Amen.

The Lord's Prayer, Fraction, *Agnus Dei*, Prayer for peace, Kiss of peace, Invitation, Communion Chant, Communion, Prayer of Thanksgiving, Blessing.

INDEX